Springer Proceedings in Complexity

Springer Proceedings in Complexity publishes proceedings from scholarly meetings on all topics relating to the interdisciplinary studies of complex systems science. Springer welcomes book ideas from authors. The series is indexed in Scopus.

Proposals must include the following:

- name, place and date of the scientific meeting
- a link to the committees (local organization, international advisors etc.)
- scientific description of the meeting
- list of invited/plenary speakers
- an estimate of the planned proceedings book parameters (number of pages/articles, requested number of bulk copies, submission deadline)

Submit your proposals to: Hisako.Niko@springer.com

Diogo Pacheco · Andreia Sofia Teixeira ·
Hugo Barbosa · Ronaldo Menezes ·
Giuseppe Mangioni
Editors

Complex Networks XIII

Proceedings of the 13th Conference on Complex Networks, CompleNet 2022

Springer

Editors
Diogo Pacheco
Department of Computer Science
University of Exeter
Exeter, UK

Hugo Barbosa
Department of Computer Science
University of Exeter
Exeter, UK

Giuseppe Mangioni
Dipartimento di Ingegneria Elettrica,
Elettronica e Informatica
University of Catania
Catania, Italy

Andreia Sofia Teixeira
LASIGE and Department of Informatics
Faculty of Sciences
Lisbon, Portugal

Ronaldo Menezes
Department of Computer Science
University of Exeter
Exeter, UK

ISSN 2213-8684 ISSN 2213-8692 (electronic)
Springer Proceedings in Complexity
https://doi.org/10.1007/978-3-031-17658-6

This Springer imprint is published by the registered company Springer Nature Switzerland AG
The registered company address is: Gewerbestrasse 11, 6330 Cham, Switzerland
(www.springernature.com/mycopy)

Contents

Targeted Attacks on the World Air Transportation Network: Impact on Its Regional Structure 1
Issa Moussa Diop, Chantal Cherifi, Cherif Diallo, and Hocine Cherifi

Measuring Equality and Hierarchical Mobility on Abstract Complex Networks 15
Matthew Russell Barnes, Vincenzo Nicosia, and Richard G. Clegg

Broadcast Graphs with Nodes of Limited Memory 29
Saber Gholami and Hovhannes A. Harutyunyan

Investigating the Origins of Fractality Based on Two Novel Fractal Network Models 43
Enikő Zakar-Polyák, Marcell Nagy, and Roland Molontay

A Data-Driven Approach to Cattle Epidemic Modelling Under Uncertainty 55
Sima Farokhnejad, Denis Cardoso, Christiane Rocha, Angélica S. da Mata, and Ronaldo Menezes

Building a Reliable, Dynamic and Temporal Synthetic Model of the World Trade Web 69
Sean Kennedy, Michael Wish, Philip Smith, James Sherrell, William Shields, and Ralucca Gera

Co-Attention Based Multi-contextual Fake News Detection 83
Paritosh Kapadia, Akrati Saxena, Bhaskarjyoti Das, Yulong Pei, and Mykola Pechenizkiy

Correlation Financial Networks of an Unstable Stock Market: Empirical Study 97
Sergei Sidorov, Alexey Faizliev, Vladimir Balash, Dmitriy Melnichuk, and Alexey Grigoriev

Extracting Characteristic Areas Based on Topic Distribution over Proximity Tree 109
Takayasu Fushimi and Emi Matsuo

Author Index 121

Contributors

Vladimir Balash Saratov State University, Saratov, Russia

Matthew Russell Barnes School of Electronic Engineering and Computer Science, Queen Mary University of London, London, UK

Denis Cardoso Department of Veterinary Medicine, Federal University of Lavras, MG, Brazil

Chantal Cherifi DISP Lab, University of Lyon 2, Lyon, France

Hocine Cherifi LIB EA 7534, University of Burgundy Franche-Comté, Dijon, France

Richard G. Clegg School of Electronic Engineering and Computer Science, Queen Mary University of London, London, UK

Angélica S. da Mata Department of Computer Science, University of Exeter, Exeter, England, UK

Bhaskarjyoti Das PES University, Bangalore, India

Cherif Diallo LACCA Lab, Gaston Berger University, Saint-Louis, Senegal

Issa Moussa Diop LACCA Lab, Gaston Berger University, Saint-Louis, Senegal

Alexey Faizliev Saratov State University, Saratov, Russia

Sima Farokhnejad Department of Computer Science, University of Exeter, Exeter, England, UK

Takayasu Fushimi School of Computer Science, Tokyo University of Technology, Hachioji, Japan

Ralucca Gera Department of Applied Mathematics, Naval Postgraduate School, Monterey, CA, USA

Saber Gholami Department of Computer Science and Software Engineering, Concordia University, Montreal, QC, Canada

Alexey Grigoriev Saratov State University, Saratov, Russia

Hovhannes A. Harutyunyan Department of Computer Science and Software Engineering, Concordia University, Montreal, QC, Canada

Paritosh Kapadia Eindhoven University of Technology, Eindhoven, The Netherlands

Sean Kennedy Department of Electrical and Computer Engineering, Naval Postgraduate School, Monterey, CA, USA

Emi Matsuo School of Computer Science, Tokyo University of Technology, Hachioji, Japan

Dmitriy Melnichuk Saratov State University, Saratov, Russia

Ronaldo Menezes Department of Computer Science, University of Exeter, Exeter, England, UK

Roland Molontay Department of Stochastics, Institute of Mathematics, Budapest University of Technology and Economics, Budapest, Hungary;
ELKH-BME Stochastics Research Group, Budapest, Hungary

Marcell Nagy Department of Stochastics, Institute of Mathematics, Budapest University of Technology and Economics, Budapest, Hungary

Vincenzo Nicosia School of Mathematical Sciences, Queen Mary University of London, London, UK

Mykola Pechenizkiy Eindhoven University of Technology, Eindhoven, The Netherlands

Yulong Pei Eindhoven University of Technology, Eindhoven, The Netherlands

Christiane Rocha Department of Veterinary Medicine, Federal University of Lavras, MG, Brazil

Akrati Saxena Eindhoven University of Technology, Eindhoven, The Netherlands

James Sherrell Department of Applied Mathematics, Naval Postgraduate School, Monterey, CA, USA

William Shields Department of Operations Research, Naval Postgraduate School, Monterey, CA, USA

Sergei Sidorov Saratov State University, Saratov, Russia

Philip Smith Department of Applied Mathematics, Naval Postgraduate School, Monterey, CA, USA

Michael Wish Department of Physics, Naval Postgraduate School, Monterey, CA, USA

Enikő Zakar-Polyák Department of Stochastics, Institute of Mathematics, Budapest University of Technology and Economics, Budapest, Hungary

Targeted Attacks on the World Air Transportation Network: Impact on Its Regional Structure

Issa Moussa Diop, Chantal Cherifi, Cherif Diallo, and Hocine Cherifi

Abstract Perturbations of the air transport network have a tremendous impact on many sectors of activity. Therefore, a better understanding of its robustness to targeted attacks is essential. The literature reports numerous investigations at different levels (world, regional, airline) considering various targeted attack strategies. However, few works consider the mesoscopic organization of the network. To fill this gap, we rely on the component structure recently introduced in the network literature. Indeed, the world air transportation network possesses seven local components capturing the regional flights in localized areas. Its global component, distributed worldwide, capture the interregional routes. We investigate the impact of two influential attacks (Degree, Betweenness) on the world air transportation network at the regional and inter-regional levels. Results show that the seven regions are isolated one after the other from the world air transportation network. Additionally, although the Betweenness attack effectively splits the network, its impact on regional routes is less pronounced.

1 Introduction

Every day, millions of passengers and frets transit by air transport. This infrastructure is essential in people's lives for economic, social, and health purposes. A disturbance can have significant consequences in different sectors of activity. Therefore, it is vital

I. M. Diop (✉) · C. Diallo
LACCA Lab, Gaston Berger University, PB 234, Saint-Louis, Senegal
e-mail: diop.issa-moussa@ugb.edu.sn

C. Diallo
e-mail: cherif.diallo@ugb.edu.sn

C. Cherifi
DISP Lab, University of Lyon 2, Lyon, France
e-mail: chantal.bonnercherifi@univ-lyon2.fr

H. Cherifi
LIB EA 7534, University of Burgundy Franche-Comté, 21078 Dijon, France
e-mail: hocine.cherifi@u-bourgogne.fr

D. Pacheco et al. (eds.), *Complex Networks XIII*, Springer Proceedings in Complexity,
https://doi.org/10.1007/978-3-031-17658-6_1

to study its disruption to limit the damage. The complex network paradigm attempts to provide solutions in this sense. Indeed, representing the airports as nodes and the flights between two airports as links, the robustness of the air transportation network has been extensively studied. One uses a random attack to account for accidental service disruption in an airport. In this case, one evaluates the impact of removing nodes at random on the network topology. Robustness studies also consider targeted attacks. In this case, the goal is to elaborate a node removal strategy to damage as much as possible the network. Besides, one can distinguish studies either linked to geographical areas (worldwide, regional, national) or airlines in the literature. To contextualize our work, we briefly describe important related works. For more details about the robustness of the air transportation network, the reader can refer to [7, 9].

In [8], the authors conduct an extensive analysis of the robustness of the world air transportation network. They use six centrality measures (Betweenness, Closeness, Eigenvector, Bonacich, and Damage) to quantify the importance of airports. They consider two attack strategies. A strong attack removes the nodes in descending order of the centrality measure, while a weak attack uses the inverse order. They perform the experiments on three networks: (1) the unweighted network, (2) the network weighted by the number of passengers, (3) the network weighted by the inverse distance between airports. They compare three robustness metrics when removing a node: (1) the size of the giant component, (2) the number of survived links, (3) the number of unaffected passengers with rerouting. Results show that the size of the giant component is not appropriate for evaluating weak attacks' robustness. Furthermore, it overestimates the robustness of strong attacks. In comparison, survived links fix these two anomalies. In addition, according to the unaffected passenger with rerouting, Degree centrality is the most effective attack when 7% of nodes are disconnected. Bonacich takes the lead when more than 7% are disconnected. The robustness is sensitive to the type of weight of the network. In [5], the authors investigate the robustness of the seven regional unweighted networks defined by the OAG (Africa, Asia, Europe, Latin America, Middle East, North America, and South Pacific). They perform strong attacks based on Degree, Betweenness, and Damage. The size of the giant component evaluates the robustness. Results show that Damage is the most effective attack for a small fraction of removed nodes. However, Betweenness performs better when the number of removed nodes grows. Results also show evidence that differences across regions are related to the size of the value of the k-core. Areas with a large core of densely connected airports, such as Europe and the Middle East, are more resilient than regions with a smaller core. In [10], the authors investigate the robustness and weighted (number of flights per week) and unweighted Belt and Road region network. Strong attacks on the unweighted network use Degree, Betweenness, Closeness, and Eigenvector centrality. For the weighted network, they investigate strong attacks based on recursive power and recursive centrality. They test four robustness metrics: clustering coefficient, average shortest path length, graph diversity, and global efficiency. Results show that the Betweenness centrality is the least robust for the clustering coefficient, average shortest path, and global efficiency for the unweighted network. The Degree is less resilient for the graph diversity. Recursive power is more sensitive to all the network properties for the weighted network. By comparing the weighted and unweighted network's robustness, no targeted attack dominates entirely. Indeed, the Betweenness centrality is less robust for the average shortest path and the graph diversity. The Degree is sensitive to graph diversity. Finally, the recursive power is less resilient for the clustering coefficient. In [6], the authors investigate the topology and robustness of unweighted networks of airlines. They study 10 Full-Service Carriers belonging to three airline alliances (Star Alliance, OneWorld, and SkyTeam) and 3 Low-Cost Carriers (Ryanair, EasyJet, and Southwest Airlines). Random and targeted strong attacks based on Degree and Betweenness centrality are performed. The size of the giant component is the robustness metric. Low-Cost Carriers are more resilient than Full-Service Carriers to random attacks, but the difference is not significant. The attack based on the Degree is more resilient than the attack based on the Betweenness. But the difference is small. The hybrid model airlines tend to be more robust than the Low-Cost Carriers airlines, which resist better targeted attacks than the Full-Service Carriers airlines.

Our work departs from previous studies. It concerns the interactions between the unweighted world air transportation network and its regional components. In earlier work, we introduced a network decomposition called the component structure of a network [2]. It decomposes a network into its local components and global components. Local components are localized dense areas of the original network. The links joining the local components and their associated nodes form the global components. Based on this representation, air world transportation comprises several regional components corresponding to natural geographic and cultural areas. The inter-regional components reveal the main airports and routes between these regions. Based on this representation, we explore the impact of targeted attacks on the world air transportation network on its regional and inter-regional components. We consider Degree and Betweenness centrality measures to remove nodes in descending order. These experiments give new insight into the interactions between international and regional routes exposed to disruption.

The rest of the paper is organized as follows. Section 2 introduces the background. Section 3 presents the data and methods. Section 4 reports the main findings of our analysis. Section 5 discusses the results and then gives conclusions.

2 Background

2.1 Component Structure

The density of real-world networks is generally not uniform. One usually captures this phenomenon using two mesoscopic features: (1) the community structure, (2) the core-periphery structure. Although there is no consensus on a universal definition of these representations, they share the fact that the network contains groups of nodes tightly connected called core or communities. They are supposed to be loosely related to other groups when considering the community structure. Peripherical nodes sharing few connections surround these core groups in the multi-core-periphery structure. The component structure builds in these representations. It splits the networks into dense groups and their interactions. One obtains the local components by isolating the dense parts of the networks. Links and nodes connecting the local components form the global components. To build the component structure one proceeds as follows:

1. Uncover the dense parts of the network.
2. Remove the links between the dense parts to extract the local components.
3. Remove the links within the dense parts and the subsequently isolated nodes to extract the global components.

Note that this representation is redundant. Indeed, a node can simultaneously belong to a local and a global component. One can use community detection or multi-core-periphery algorithms to extract the dense parts of the network. We consider an approach based on the community structure to extract the components in this work Fig. 1. A describes the extraction process of the component structure. In this example, one uses a non-overlapping community detection algorithm to extract the dense parts of the network. Then, we form the local components by removing the inter-community links. Removing the intra-community links and the isolated nodes extracts the global components.

2.2 *Targeted Attack*

Targeted attacks aim to remove the most vital nodes for network connectivity [1]. Centrality measures generally describe the importance of nodes [4]. In a strong attack strategy, one removes nodes in the network in descending order of magnitude of the chosen centrality. This work uses the most popular measures: Degree and Betweenness.

Degree centrality of a node is the number of its first-order neighbors. Given a graph $G(V, E)$, such as V is the set of nodes and E the set of links, the Degree k_i of node i is defined as:

$$k_i = \sum_{j \in V, i \neq j} a_{ij}$$

a_{ij} is an element of the binary adjacency matrix of G such as $a_{ij} = 1$ if i and j are connected, otherwise, $a_{ij} = 0$.

Betweenness centrality of a node is the fraction of the shortest path passing through it. When it is normalized, the Betweenness of the node i is defined as:

$$b(i) = \frac{2}{(n-1)(n-2)} \sum_{i \neq j} \frac{\sigma_{jk(i)}}{\sigma_{jk}}$$

σ_{jk} is the number of the shortest path between j and k. $\sigma_{jk}(i)$ is the number of the shortest path from j to k passing in i.

2.3 *Evaluation Measures*

The size of the giant component is the most popular metric to assess the robustness of a network. It refers to the size of the largest set of interconnected nodes when the network brakes into several parts due to node removal. The higher the size of the giant component, the most resilient the network is to the attack.

3 Data and Methods

3.1 *Data*

We consider an unweighted and undirected network originating from FlightAware [3]. Flight information has been collected for six days (between May 17, 2018, and May 22, 2018). Nodes represent airports, and links represent direct flights between airports during the period. Table 1 reports its basic topological properties.

3.2 *Methods*

Our goal is to evaluate the impact of a targeted attack on the world route network on its regional and inter-regional constituents. Therefore, once the component structure is extracted, the robustness evaluation process proceeds as follows:

1. Disconnect the node from the world air transportation network according to an attack strategy.
2. Disconnect the same node from its local component.
3. Disconnect the same node from the global component if it also belongs.
4. Extract the giant component from the world air transportation network.
5. Extract the giant component from the concerned local component.
6. Extract the giant component from the global component.

This approach allows us to visualize the impact of removing a critical airport in the world air transportation network on the robustness of the regional and inter-regional networks. Figure 1b reports a toy example illustrating an attack on an airport of the world network and the disruptions induced in the local and global components of the network.

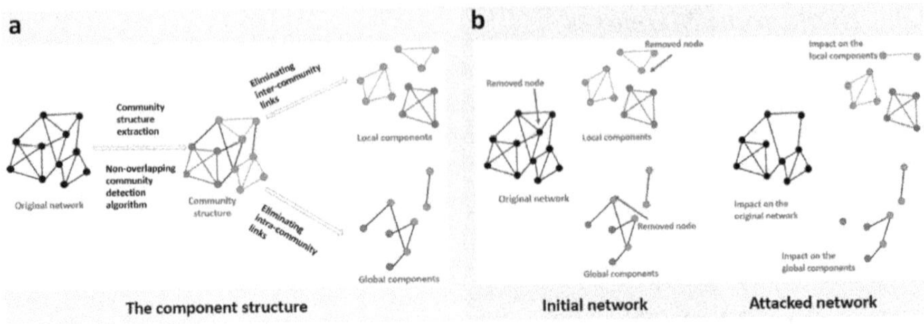

Fig. 1 **a** Process to uncover the component structure. The community structure is used for example, to extract the dense parts **b** Attack on the network

4 Experimental Results

4.1 Component Structure

We rely on the Louvain community detection algorithm to uncover the dense parts of the network. Indeed, communities are tightly connected nodes. It reveals 27 communities. Therefore, we consider that there are 27 local components. There are seven large and twenty small components localized in various geographical areas. The largest local components cover the following regions: (1) North America-Caribbean, (2) Europe, (3) East and Southeast Asia, (4) Africa-Middle East-Southern Asia, (5) Oceania, (6) South America, (7) Russia-Central Asia-Transcaucasia. Note that this subdivision is different than the partition proposed by the OAG (Official Airline Guide) used in [5].

There are fifteen global components. The largest one regroups more than 96% of the airports, and it is distributed over the world [2]. Figure 2 represents the airports included in the largest local and global components. We restrict our attention to the seven largest local components and the main global component in the following robustness analysis. Table 1 reports their basic topological properties.

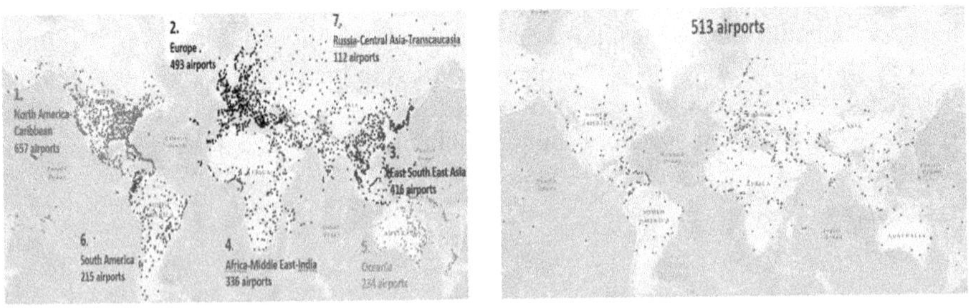

Fig. 2 Left figure: The airports in the seven large local components. Each color represent a component. Right figure: The largest global component

Table 1 Basic topological properties of the world air transportation network, the 7 large local components, and the largest global component. N is the network size. $|E|$ is the number of edges. $diam$ is the diameter. l is the average shortest path length. ν is the density. ζ is the transitivity also called global clustering coefficient. $k_{nn}(k)$ is the assortativity also called Degree correlation coefficient. η is the hub dominance

Components	N	$\|E\|$	$diam$	l	ν	ζ	$k_{nn}(k)$	η
World air transportation network	2734	16665	12	3,86	0,004	0,26	−0,05	0.09
North America-Caribbean	657	3828	7	2.88	0.018	0.28	−0.325	0.29
Europe	493	5181	6	2.58	0.042	0.32	−0.2	0.33
East and Southeast Asia	416	2495	7	2.9	0.029	0.34	−0.22	0.32
Africa-Middle East-India	337	1197	6	3.25	0.021	0.28	−0.15	0.23
Oceania	234	464	9	3.5	0.017	0.18	−0.22	0.24
South America	215	527	6	3.15	0.023	0.23	−0.35	0.22
Russia-Central Asia-Transcaucasia	112	427	4	2.23	0.07	0.23	−0.39	0.73
Large global component	513	2194	8	3.28	0.017	0.13	−0.25	0.2

4.2 Degree Targeted Attack

Figure 3a illustrates the evolution of the LCC with the fraction of top Degree nodes removed from the world air transportation network in descending order of the airports' Degree centrality. We also plot the induced evolution of the LCC of the various large components. All the curves exhibit similar behavior. As the fraction of nodes removed from the world air transportation network grows, the LCC of the components decreases almost linearly. Overall, the European component is the most resilient. The East and Southeast Asia components and the World Air Transportation Network follow. They behave similarly when the fraction of removed nodes is below 5%. Beyond this value, the gap between the evolution of their LCC with the European component widens. Africa-Middle East-Southern, Russia-Central Asia-Transcaucasia, and the largest global components form a group of overlapping curves when the fraction of removed nodes is below 7.5%. Beyond this value, they diverge. The North America-Caribbean component follows. Finally, Oceania and South America components are the most sensitive to the attack. Indeed, their LCC breaks down to 33% and 28% respectively, after removing around 4.7% of the airports. A more detailed observation shows two types of behavior. In the first case, the LCC exhibits piecewise linear variations. It concerns South America, Oceania, and Russia-Central Asia-Transcaucasia. Removing a particular node produces a sharp drop in the LCC because an entire subnetwork broke away from the primary component, causing considerable damage.

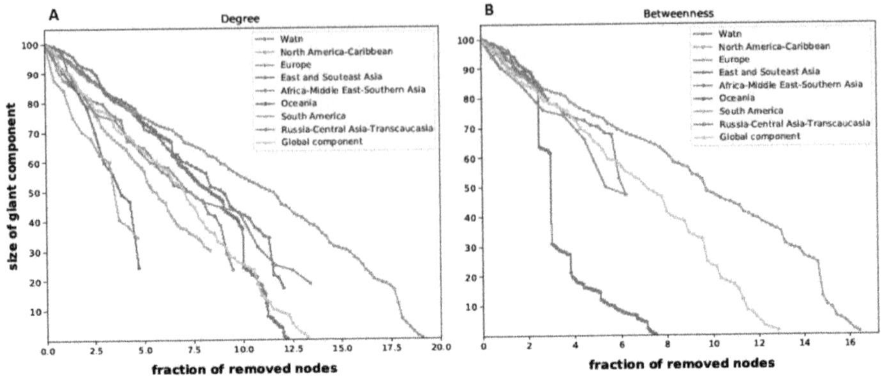

Fig. 3 The size of the giant component of the world air transportation network, and the large components as a function of removed nodes under targeted attacks on the world air transportation network

In contrast, in the other components and the world air transportation network, the size of the LCC varies almost linearly with the fraction of removed nodes. The same proportion of nodes leaves the LCC, whatever the node removed in this situation.

We now look at when the components become isolated from the world air transportation network. We identify the critical airport disconnecting the component. We explore the topological properties of the remaining regional network to evaluate the impact on the regional traffic. Table 2 displays the basic topological properties of the components after isolation.

Oceania is the first component to separate from the world air transportation network. It occurs after removing 9% of the top Degree nodes from the world air transportation network. The proportion of top Degree nodes of this component subtracted before the split equals 4.7%. Christchurch, in New Zealand, is the last top-Degree airport removed, provoking the separation. Only 24% of the airports remain in the LCC of this component. They are all in Australia. All the other countries are unreachable. Although the LCC is denser than the initial component, traveling in this region becomes more challenging. Indeed, Table 2 shows that the diameter and the average shortest path increase, and the transitivity decrease. The North America-Caribbean local component is the second to break away after removing 9.7% of the top Degree nodes from the world air transportation network. When it happens, 8.4% top Degree airports in this component have already been removed. Winnipeg /James A Richardson Airport in Canada is the last airport connecting the region to the world before the split. In contrast to Oceania, airports in the LCC are distributed in the different countries of the component. However, Alaska is isolated, and in Canada, there are only a few airports in Quebec and Ontario. The remaining LCC contains 30% of the airports of the initial component. Table 2 shows that travels in the region become uneasy. Indeed, eight hops on average and 21 at maximum are required to join any two airports. In addition, density and transitivity decrease.

Table 2 Basic topological properties of the 7 large isolated local components after the attack based on the Degree. *LCC* is the Largest Connected Component. $|E|$ is the number of edges. *diam* is the diameter. l is the average shortest path length. ν is the density. ζ is the transitivity also called global clustering coefficient. $k_{nn}(k)$ is the assortativity also called Degree correlation coefficient

Components	LCC	$\|E\|$	$diam$	l	ν	ζ	$k_{nn}(k)$	$LCC(\%)$
North America-Caribbean	196	301	21	7.22	0.015	0.21	−0.14	29.8
Europe	136	177	13	5.75	0.019	0.07	−0.13	27.5
East and Southeast Asia	72	104	11	4.51	0.04	0.18	−0.15	17.2
Africa-Middle East-India	79	110	17	6.9	0.035	0.26	−0.08	23.5
Oceania	57	65	15	5.1	0.04	0.12	−0.2	24.3
South America	74	98	13	5.7	0.036	0.21	−0.43	34.4
Russia-Central Asia-Transcaucasia	21	28	6	2.85	0.13	0.08	−0.11	18.7

Disconnecting 9.8% of the airports in the global air network is sufficient to isolate the South America component. A proportion of 4.6% top Degree nodes are removed from the component before separation. Salgado Filho Airport (Brazil) is the last link with the rest of the world before the break. The LCC contains 34% of the airports of the initial component. Most of its airports are in Brazil and its neighboring countries. Argentina is unreachable. Even though it is denser than the initial component, the shortest path and the diameter reveal that this network doesn't facilitate the traffic (see Table 2). Note that the transitivity doesn't fluctuate much. The next component that becomes unreachable is East and Southeast Asia. It breaks away after removing almost 11% of the top hubs from the overall network. Before the split, 12% of the top Degree nodes of this component have been removed. Gimhae Airport in South Korea is the last airport reachable before separation. The LCC contains 17% of the airports from the initial component. They are mainly in China and its satellite countries. Compared to the other isolated component, it is the easiest to travel, even though its transitivity is low. One needs to eliminate 11.2% of the high Degree airports of the world air network to isolate the Africa-Middle East-Southern Asia region. The targeted hubs include 9.5% of the airports of this component. The Benazir Bhutto Airport in Pakistan is the last connected to other areas in the world. The LCC contains 23.5% of the airports of the initial component. They are located mainly in West-Central Africa and India. Traveling into the LCC is difficult even though it is denser than the original component. Almost all the Middle East, South Africa, and East of Africa airports are unreachable. Moreover, a maximum of 17 hops are required to join any two airports, while on average, it is seven hops. Russia-Central Asia-Transcaucasia is the next component to separate from the world air transportation network. One needs to remove 11.4% of the top hubs of the world, including 13.4% of this component's hubs. The last removed airport, the Heydar Aliyev Airport, is in Azerbaijan. Only

18.7% of the airports initially in the component remains in the LCC. Except for two airports located in Uzbekistan and Tajikistan, All the others are in Russia. Compared to the initial component, the topological properties do not change much. Traveling in what remains of the component is as easy. Once Russia-Central Asia-Transcaucasia is isolated, all the airports remaining in the world air transportation are in Europe. It occurs after removing 19% of the top Degree nodes of the Europe component. The LCC contains 27.5% of the airports of the original component located in various countries. However, countries like Spain, Norway, Sweden, and Finland are almost unreachable. It is more difficult to travel within the LCC than in the initial component. Indeed, the diameter and the average shortest path values double. In addition, the density and the transitivity decrease significantly. Finally, there are no more routes in the world air transportation network after removing 12.2% of its most influential airports.

4.3 Betweenness Targeted Attack

Figure 3b displays the variation of the LLC as a function of the fraction of top Betweenness centrality airports removed from the world air transportation network. We also plot the corresponding evolution for the components. Removing up to 3% of top airports does not significantly differ in the various components. Indeed, the curves are very close. Nevertheless, Africa-Middle East-Southern Asia, East and Southeast Asia, and Europe are slightly more resilient. Above this value, Europe appears clearly as the most robust component. One can still distinguish the two types of behavior observed in the previous experiment. The LCC varies almost linearly in the Europe component and to a lesser extent in the global component. Piecewise linear variation with sharp drops characterizes the others and, more particularly, the World air transportation network.

South America is the first isolated area after removing 1.6% of the world's major airports. The last link with the World is Comodoro A M Benítez airport in Chili. Only two airports in this region are in the top 1.6% world airports (Guarulhos-Governador, André F Montoro in Brazil, and Comodoro A M Benítez airport in Chili). The LCC contains 93.5% of the airports of the initial component scattered in all the countries. The topological properties of the LCC do not change significantly as compared to the initial component, and the regional traffic keeps its efficiency. Removing 2.1% of the top airports disconnect Oceania from the world transportation network. Perth airport is the last connection before isolation. Only one airport (Sydney K Smith) before Perth has been targeted before isolation. The LCC retains 90.2% of the airports from the initial component across all its countries. The topological properties do not change much, and the internal travels in this component are not much disturbed. East and Southeast Asia is the next component to become unreachable from the other parts of the world after removing 2.3% of the world's most important airports. Among them, there are 2.6% of the airports in this region. The last connection is through the Kunming Changshui Airport in China. The LCC contains 82.4% of the airports initially in the component. They are located in the various countries of this component. Compared to the initial component, the topological properties of the LCC are comparable. Therefore, the impact of the isolation on regional routes is limited. North America-Caribbean is the fourth isolated area. It becomes unreachable after removing 2.9% of the top central world airports. Among these, there are the top 2.9% of this component. Simón Bolívar Airport in Venezuela is the last liaison to the world before isolation. The LCC contains 79.6% of the airports still interconnected. Note that the Alaska subregion is inaccessible. The LCC is a bit less efficient than the component. Indeed, it keeps some large hubs, except in Canada. The topological properties of the LCC indicate that it is more challenging to travel than in the initial network. The next isolated area is the Africa-Middle East-Southern Asia, when one removes 3.9% of the central airports from the world network. Around 5.6% of the airports from this component are the target of the attack. As for the Degree centrality, Benazir Bhutto Airport in Pakistan is the last removed. The LCC maintains 47.6% of the airports in this region connected. Once again, the Middle East and the Horn of Africa are the most impacted. They are almost unreachable. Traveling within this region becomes difficult. Indeed, the diameter (14 hops) and the average shortest path (6 hops) of the LCC are two times higher. The density and the transitivity are comparable with the initial component values. Russia-Central Asia-Transcaucasia is the next region to break away from the world network after removing the top 5% central airports of the global air transportation network. The attack involves 6.2% major airports of this component before the separation. They are mainly in Russia. The last removed airport is Krasnodar Pashkovsky Airport. The size of the LCC reduces to 47.3% of the initial component. Comparing its topological properties to the initial component allows us to conclude that the impact on regional easiness to travel is limited. After splitting with Russia-Central Asia-Transcaucasia, Europe preserves 61.8% of its airports in the LCC. They are scattered in all the countries of the initial component. Compared to the latter, the LCC is less dense. In addition, one requires more hops to join any two airports (Table 3).

5 Discussion and Conclusion

In this work, we leverage the component structure of the world air transportation network to analyze the impact of targeted attacks on the regional and inter-regional routes. We consider attacks based on two influential centrality measures. The first one, based on Degree, removes nodes according to their number of connections in descending order. The second one uses the proportion of shortest paths transiting through a node to rank the nodes. We perform the experiments on an undirected and unweighted network to focus on routes rather than flights or passengers.

Results show that whatever the attack on the world air transportation network, one can link the way the network disintegrates to the component structure. Indeed, components get isolated one after the other when removing a certain proportion of the top centrality nodes from the world air transportation network. The main differ-

Table 3 Basic topological properties of the 7 large isolated local components after the attack based on the Betweenness. LCC is the Largest Connected Component. $|E|$ is the number of edges. $diam$ is the diameter. l is the average shortest path length. ν is the density. ζ is the transitivity also called global clustering coefficient. $k_{nn}(k)$ is the assortativity also called Degree correlation coefficient

Components	LCC	$\|E\|$	$diam$	l	ν	ζ	$k_{nn}(k)$	$LCC(\%)$
North America-Caribbean	523	1918	8	3.23	0.14	0.2	−0.27	79.6
Europe	305	1252	8	3.39	0.027	0.16	0.014	61.8
East and Southeast Asia	343	1421	8	3.51	0.24	0.32	−0.11	82.4
Africa-Middle East-India	160	290	14	5.29	0.022	0.26	−0.25	47.6
Oceania	211	383	9	3.6	0.017	0.17	−0.21	90.2
South America	201	449	7	3.32	0.022	0.21	−0.38	93.5
Russia-Central Asia-Transcaucasia	53	105	5	2.84	0.07	0.2	−0.32	47.32

ences between the two types of attack are the fraction of top removed nodes needed for a component to break away from the world network and the size of the remaining isolated component. Globally, one needs to target more nodes before isolation in the Degree attack than the Betweenness attack. Furthermore, the isolated components' size is smaller in the Degree of attack. Indeed, it prioritizes the top internal hubs in the components, reducing their size. One needs to remove many internal high Degree nodes before reaching the inter-regional airports tying the components together. In contrast, Betweenness centrality focuses on inter-regional airports, splitting earlier the components with minor damage to their internal structure. One after the other, South America, Oceania, East, Southeast Asia, and North America are isolated regions by the Betweenness attack. Oceania, North America, South America, and East and Southeast Asia leave the world network in this order when targeting nodes by Degree centrality. Then Africa-Middle East-Southern Asia, followed by Russia-Central Asia-Transcaucasia separate from Europe in the two attack strategies. Note that economic and geographic ties connect these two groups of regions.

The component structure allows us to study the robustness of the world air transportation network from a new perspective. Indeed, it is a mixture of subnetworks with various internal densities geographically well identified. Looking at its robustness through its component structure allows us to highlight the impact of targeted attacks in different world areas. These results will enable us to tailor the protection strategies to maintain inter-regional routes and minimize the effect of disruption at the regional level. Future work will also consider developing more effective attack strategies based on the component structure.

References

1. Chakraborty, D., Singh, A., Cherifi, H.: Immunization strategies based on the overlapping nodes in networks with community structure. In: International Conference on Computational Social Networks, pp. 62–73. Springer, Cham (2016)
2. Diop, I.M., Cherifi, C., Diallo, C., Cherifi, H.: Revealing the component structure of the world air transportation network. Appl. Netw. Sci. **6**(1), 1–50 (2021)
3. Flightaware (2018). https://flightaware.com/
4. Ibnoulouafi, A., El Haziti, M., Cherifi, H.: M-centrality: identifying key nodes based on global position and local degree variation. J. Stat. Mech.: Theory Exp. **2018**(7), 073407 (2018)
5. Lordan, O., Sallan, J.M.: Core and critical cities of global region airport networks. Phys. Stat. Mech. Appl. **513**, 724–733 (2019)
6. Lordan, O., Sallan, J.M., Escorihuela, N., Gonzalez-Prieto, D.: Robustness of airline route networks. Phys. Stat. Mech. Appl. **445**, 18–26 (2016)
7. Lordan, O., Sallan, J.M., Simo, P.: Study of the topology and robustness of airline route networks from the complex network approach: a survey and research agenda. J. Transp. Geogr. **37**, 112–120 (2014)
8. Sun, X., Gollnick, V., Wandelt, S.: Robustness analysis metrics for worldwide airport network: a comprehensive study. Chin. J. Aeronaut. **30**(2), 500–512 (2017)
9. Sun, X., Wandelt, S.: Robustness of air transportation as complex networks: systematic review of 15 years of research and outlook into the future. Sustainability **13**(11), 6446 (2021)
10. Zhang, L., Zhao, Y., Chen, D., Zhang, X.: Analysis of network robustness in weighted and unweighted approaches: a case study of the air transport network in the belt and road region. J. Adv. Transp. **2021** (2021)

References

Measuring Equality and Hierarchical Mobility on Abstract Complex Networks

Matthew Russell Barnes, Vincenzo Nicosia, and Richard G. Clegg

Abstract The centrality of a node within a network, however it is measured, is a vital proxy for the importance or influence of that node, and the differences in node centrality generate hierarchies and inequalities. If the network is evolving in time, the influence of each node changes in time as well, and the corresponding hierarchies are modified accordingly. However, there is still a lack of systematic study into the ways in which the centrality of a node evolves when a graph changes. In this paper we introduce a taxonomy of metrics of equality and hierarchical mobility in networks that evolve in time. We propose an indicator of equality based on the classical Gini Coefficient from economics, and we quantify the hierarchical mobility of nodes, that is, how and to what extent the centrality of a node and its neighbourhood change over time. These measures are applied to a corpus of thirty time evolving network data sets from different domains. We show that the proposed taxonomy measures can discriminate between networks from different fields. We also investigate correlations between different taxonomy measures, and demonstrate that some of them have consistently strong correlations (or anti-correlations) across the entire corpus. The mobility and equality measures developed here constitute a useful toolbox for investigating the nature of network evolution, and also for discriminating between different artificial models hypothesised to explain that evolution.

1 Introduction

Hierarchies exist in every facet of our daily lives and understanding their ordering and dynamics is important to discern patterns and enable informed comparisons. A recent paper [15] studies how rankings evolve over time and the universal dynamics of hierarchies. In our work we apply a similar approach in the context of networks

M. R. Barnes (✉) · R. G. Clegg
School of Electronic Engineering and Computer Science, Queen Mary University of London, London, UK
e-mail: matthew.barnes@qmul.ac.uk

V. Nicosia
School of Mathematical Sciences, Queen Mary University of London, London, UK

D. Pacheco et al. (eds.), *Complex Networks XIII*, Springer Proceedings in Complexity,
https://doi.org/10.1007/978-3-031-17658-6_2

that evolve in time. The analysis of time evolving networks traditionally consists of tracking the evolution of network statistics such as degree distribution, clustering coefficient, assortativity and diameter. However, these overall statistics usually do not capture how individual nodes change their position within hierarchies, i.e., how their "status" improves or deteriorates over time.

In this paper we look at networks evolving in time, from the perspective of individual nodes, and we study how the characteristics of such nodes change as the network changes, with a special focus on degree centrality. A node's degree could be considered as a measure of its status or importance e.g. the number of citations in a citation network [25] or friends in a social network. Obviously, not all nodes in a network have the same importance, and their roles can change over time as a result of the evolution of the network. Equality is a classical measure to quantify whether nodes tend to have the same centrality as other nodes, or whether centrality is concentrated in some nodes and not others. Similarly, hierarchical mobility measures whether nodes are frozen in their hierarchy position of high or low centrality. It is particularly interesting to consider how equality and hierarchical mobility evolve as a network changes.[1]

Consider the Barabási–Albert (BA) model [1] and the Fortunato model [8] both of which produce power law degree distributions. In the Fortunato model a node attracts new nodes with a probability inversely proportional to the order of its arrival in the network. In BA that probability is proportional to the current degree of the node. Consider an instantiation of a BA model G_B and a separate instantiation of a Fortunato model G_F. In both realisations, a node s arriving earlier than a node t has an advantage in gaining links. Imagine in both that t by chance gains more nodes than s. In G_B it is likely to continue to gain advantage over s but in G_F the node s will retain its higher likelihood of gaining nodes. In G_B, therefore, this change of ranking where t overtakes s, if it occurs, is more likely to be permanent.

Further to this we extend the focus to the importance of an individual node's neighbourhood, and measure this by taking the mean degree of all nodes in said neighbourhood. The interaction between nodes can be somewhat measured by the impact a node has on its neighbourhood's mean degree over time. Consider node n which at t_1 is in a neighbourhood with a smaller than average mean degree and at t_2 is in a neighbourhood with a larger than average mean degree. Does this growth for the neighbourhood correlate with node n itself having a large degree?

To look at equality we borrow the concept of the Gini coefficient [11] from classical economics which is generally used to measure wealth or income disparity. Traditional measures of economic or social mobility proved unsuitable for the setting of time evolving networks, hence we developed a taxonomy of six hierarchical mobility measures. These measures correlate the degree of individual nodes and their neighbourhoods between different points in time (see Sect. 3).

To consider these measures on real network data we collected a corpus of 30 networks that evolve in time from a number of online sources. The code used to

[1] We introduce the term hierarchical mobility to avoid confusion with the word "mobility" alone, commonly used in spatial networks as a measure of nodes' ability to move in geographic space.

collect this data and analyse it for this paper is freely available under an open source licence.[2] The networks are classified by their field and by structural properties.We used our equality measure and our taxonomy of mobility measures on this corpus to look for common patterns arising in different classes of networks. For example, we correlate the degree of a node at time t_1 with its change in neighbourhood mean degree between $[t_1, t_2]$. We call this *philanthropy* as it can be thought of as measuring whether a large degree node helps its neighbours gain degree. Each network in our corpus can be classified by its equality, and the six measures in our mobility taxonomy. We used these seven dimensions to discriminate between different fields of study in complex networks.

We performed a principal component analysis and produced a "taxonomy landscape" plot within which networks types can be differentiated. Further, we plotted each taxonomy aspect's change over time for all of the networks in the corpus. Again, this produced plots which show many how the networks can be differentiated based on our taxonomy.

The measures introduced in this paper are a new tool for giving insight into how networks behave. For example, by looking at how networks evolve in time over our seven dimension we can see which networks have ossified into a pattern of behaviour and which networks change how they evolve. Most networks in our corpus exhibit a mostly static degree hierarchy but, to our surprise, some exhibited a somewhat mobile degree hierarchy. There were large differences in equality between the networks in our corpus but the majority of networks we studied became more unequal over time.

2 Related Work

2.1 *Individual Influence on Status Hierarchy Evolution*

Abstract networks that evolve in time are an attempt to model the changes in real networks. The beginning of the pursuit for universal dynamics in the time evolution of such growing networks is often attributed to the famous Barabási-Albert (BA) [1] model. Their model replicates power-law degree distributions using simple evolution rules.

A more abstract approach was taken recently in [15] where the universal dynamics of ranking was explored for empirical systems. Through observing the dynamics of the ordered list, the authors built a framework consisting of only two key types; replacement and displacement. Either ranks are "swapped" at long ranges in the hierarchy, or ranks "diffuse" slowly between close by ranks. Their modelling approach consisted of calculating the probability of every individual to change rank to any other rank, and determined this to be monotonically increasing for "open" systems

[2] The code and data set collection information is stored here https://github.com/matthewrussellbarnes/mobility_taxonomy.

and symmetric for systems which are less open. Openness represents how fast new individuals to the system get into the top 100 ranks.

Approaches focusing on how networks evolve are becoming more numerous and many approaches try to replicate measured evolution dynamics. For instance, both [7] and [21] take the approach of measuring the effect node longevity has on its degree. It was found that a model which mimicked the preferential attachment of BA, but only for newly arrived nodes, did well in replicating the observed relationship between nodes and edges.

Another example is [34] which focused on mimicking the evolution of assortativity in social networks by calculating the probabilities of every node to be connected to k neighbours at time t. From this they derived an analytical model for calculating the assortativity of a network throughout its lifetime, and found the model was a good fit with real social network data sets.

2.2 *Equality*

Determining the distribution of finite resources among many actors in a system is a useful metric for understanding whether such resources are being concentrated or spread out. In both sociology and economics this has been a popular area of interest with each concentrating on the distribution of "status" in societies. Economists use financial income as a quantifiable proxy for status, whereas sociologists tend to keep the definition more broad and qualitative.

A common measure of equality used by economists is the Gini coefficient [11] which is derived with reference to the Lorenz curve [19], a plot of wealth versus population. The Gini coefficient G is given by

$$G = \frac{\sum_{i=1}^{n} \sum_{j=1}^{n} |x_i - x_j|}{2n^2\overline{x}} \tag{1}$$

where x_i is the income of person i, n is the number of people, and $\overline{x}$ is their mean income. This makes tracking changes in the equality measurements of populations a simple calculation. However, it does remove nuance from the result as it is a single number.

In sociology, one growing area of research has been network effects on inequality of status in social networks [12]. Much of the focus is aimed at how peer influence and network homophily [5] are large contributors to contagion of "practices" which improve a person's status.

Our approach is to measure the Gini coefficient of the distribution of degree as it evolves over time.

2.3 Hierarchical Mobility

Tracking the mobility of status hierarchies over generations has also been a focus of Sociologists and Economists. Hierarchical mobility is the amount of movement individuals experience between hierarchy levels, and the hierarchies chosen depend on the focus of interest.

Sociological hierarchies focus on occupational classes [28] which are qualitative in nature and therefore have only a subjective [6] direction of hierarchy so do not apply to our purely network topology approach. An example mobility measurement is the "Log-Multiplicative Layer Effect Model" [2] which compares two matrices (called "layers" or "generations") of class associations by assuming a uniform multiplicative association. This uniform association removes much of the much needed nuance between inter-generational class associations.

Economic hierarchies are built out of financial income bands [20] which are quantifiable and so readily ranked. A widely used mobility measurement used in economics is the Pearson correlation coefficient [26] $\beta = r(\ln Y_c, \ln Y_p)$ where $r(X, Y)$ is the Pearson correlation between numerical series X and Y. This is usually used in conjunction with $\ln Y_c = \alpha + \beta_p \ln Y_p + \epsilon_c$ where Y_c is the income of children, and Y_p is the income of parents, α is a constant and ϵ_c is a fitted constant.

Our proxy for status in abstract networks is degree centrality which, like income bands, has a definite hierarchical direction. Instead of imposing arbitrary generations we study the evolution between two points in time t_1 and t_2. In Sect. 3, we introduce more details of translating these hierarchical mobility measurements into our taxonomy of hierarchical mobility.

3 Measuring Equality and Hierarchical Mobility in Networks

3.1 Equality

Using (1) we can substitute in the degree of each node as x_i, the mean degree as $\overline{x}$ and the number of nodes as n. This is done at many time-steps throughout the life of a network and then the resulting coefficients are plotted against time to see how equality changes.

The income hierarchies used in economic analysis are very similar to degree in that they are numeric and a larger number is assumed to be a good proxy for status. However, the income of individuals fluctuate over their lifetime, both gaining and losing income. Our formulation of growing networks contain nodes that only ever increase their degree. This does not affect the calculation of equality, and moreover it allows for greater inference.

If a network is gaining a larger equality over time then the range of degree of nodes is getting narrower. As the networks are always growing it can be inferred in

Table 1 The taxonomy of mobility related aspects

Correlation	Change in degree	Mean neighbour degree	Change in mean neighbour degree
Degree	Mobility	Assortativity	Philanthropy
Change in degree		Community	Change in assortativity
Mean neighbour degree			Neighbour mobility

this case that high degree nodes are connecting to low degree more preferentially. Conversely, a lowering of equality over time suggests a divide in the connections being created. It can be inferred that lower degree nodes are more likely to attach to higher degree nodes, and less likely between themselves.

3.2 *Mobility Taxonomy*

As mentioned earlier, classical notions of social and economic mobility were not a good fit for the context of time evolving networks. To this end we introduced new measures that depend on the centrality of a node and how it evolves. In this work we consider only degree centrality.

To calculate the mobility of a node we consider the degree centrality of every node at time t_1 and the change of centrality in the period $[t_1, t_2]$. If these are highly correlated it indicates that the nodes with highest centrality at t_1 gain the most in the period to t_2. We measure this correlation using the Pearson correlation coefficient and refer to this measure as mobility.[3]

We also extended this to look at the mean centrality of each node's neighbours at time t_1 and the mean gain of centrality for this same neighbour set in the period $[t_1, t_2]$. This gives us four measures: node degree, change in node degree, mean neighbourhood degree and change in mean neighbourhood degree. Looking at the correlations between each of these gives us a taxonomy of six different mobility measures which are tabulated in Table 1.

Correlating degree at time t_1 with the change in average neighbourhood degree to t_2 can be thought of as measuring how much a high status node helps its neighbours and we call this *philanthropy*. The correlation between neighbour mean degree at t_1 and the change in the period $[t_1, t_2]$ can be thought of as *neighbourhood mobility*. The correlation between a neighbourhood's mean degree at time t_1 and a node's gain in degree between $[t_1, t_2]$ could be considered as a measure of how much neighbourhood helps a node and we refer to it as *community*. The correlation between a node's degree and its neighbours' mean degree at t_1 is the well known *assortativity*. The correlation

[3] Technically this should be called "anti"-mobility as a larger correlation coefficient refers to fewer changes in hierarchical position.

between a node's change of degree and its neighbours' mean degree between $[t_1, t_2]$ can therefore be thought of as *change in assortativity*.[4] These six measures together form a taxonomy for investigating how individual nodes and their neighbours interact and change over time.

4 Data Set Corpus

To empirically measure the prevalence of each aspect of our taxonomy in many different types of network, we have collected 30 real networks. We have assigned each data set a type based on where the data has been collected, i.e social or transportation, and information about where to find them is available under an open source licence.[5] Furthermore, we assigned each a category taken from the structural characteristics of the networks themselves, such as bipartite or the nature of newly joining nodes. For instance, citation networks grow by adding stars every iteration, i.e one node connected to all those it cites. The networks vary in size from 138 edges to nearly 1 million.[6] All networks are treated as undirected and unweighted with added links never removed.

5 Results and Discussion

5.1 Equality

We plot the Gini Coefficient (GC) of all our corpus networks on the same axis and colour the data set based on the datatype shown in Table 2. The x-axis in Fig. 1 is normalised time where the maximum duration of each network has been normalised to be between [0, 1], and 100 snapshots of equality have been calculated throughout the network's lifetime. The y-axis shows the GC, where a higher value corresponds to a lower level of equality for the network.

In Fig. 1 the GC takes values over most of the possible range (0, 1) with the values being contained between 0.2 and 0.8 from normalised time 0.2 onwards. Of the 30 data sets studied all but 4 rise in GC (becoming more unequal) between normalised time 0.0 and 1.0. The figure also shows some discrimination between the types of networks, for example social networks in general are most the unequal and contact networks most equal.

---

[4] This is not quite correct as the assortativity at t_2 would be measured on the neighbourhood set at t_2 not the neighbourhood set at t_1.

[5] See footnote 2.

[6] Some networks were originally above 1 million edges but here are truncated to keep computational time reasonable.

Table 2 Data sets used for network creation, limited to 1 million edges

	Name	Description	Type	Structure	Nodes	Edges
a	College Messages [22]	Messages between students on a UC-Irvine message board	Social	Star	1,881	13,695
b	SCOTUS Majority [9]	Legal citations among majority opinions by SCOTUS	Citation	Star	33,442	199,374
c	Amazon Ratings [18]	Amazon user connects to all products they have rated	Economic	Bipartite	743,018	975,429
d	Apostles Bible [14]	Characters in the Holy Bible's Acts of Apostles	Co-occurrence	Individual	75	160
e	Appollonius [14]	Characters in The Life of Apllonius of Tyana	Co-occurrence	Individual	92	138
f	Citations US Patents [13]	Citations among patents in the United States	Citation	Star	777,527	999,632
g	Classical Piano [24]	Transitions of chords in western classical piano music	Co-occurrence	Individual	141,571	501,033
h	Email EU [23]	E-mails between users at an EU research institution	Social	Star	986	16,006
i	Procurement EU [33]	Public EU procurement contracts	Economic	Bipartite	330,049	566,369
j	Facebook Wall [32]	Posts by users on other users' Facebook wall	Social	Star	45,580	181,666
k	Lord Of the Rings [3]	Character co-occurrence in Lord of the Rings Trilogy	Co-occurrence	Individual	139	634
l	Luke Bible [14]	Characters in the Holy Bible's Luke Gospel	Co-occurrence	Individual	76	203
n	PhD Exchange [29]	Exchange of PhD mathematicians between unis in the US	Citation	Star	230	3,643

(continued)

Table 2 (continued)

	Name	Description	Type	Structure	Nodes	Edges
o	Programming Languages [30]	Influence relationships among programming languages	Citation	Star	366	759
p	Reuters Terror News [4]	Word co-use in Reuters 9/11 coverage	Co-occurrence	Individual	13,265	146,985
q	Route Views [3]	Route Views internet topology	Computer	Individual	33,644	94,075
r	Reddit Hyperlinks Body [17]	Subreddit-to-subreddit hyperlinks from body of posts	Social	Clique	35,592	123,394
s	Reddit Hyperlinks Title [17]	Subreddit-to-subreddit hyperlinks from title of posts	Social	Individual	53,747	217,986
t	Hospital [31]	Contacts between everyone in a hospital ward	Contact	Spatial	75	1,132
u	Hypertext Conference [16]	Contacts among attendees of ACM Hypertext 2009	Contact	Spatial	113	2,192
v	Infectious [16]	Contacts during Infectious SocioPatterns 2011 event	Contact	Spatial	10,844	43,951
w	Office [10]	Contacts between individuals in an office building	Contact	Spatial	92	754
x	Primary School [27]	Contacts among students and teachers at a primary school	Contact	Spatial	242	8,298
y	AskUbuntu [23]	User answers or comments on questions on AskUbuntu	Social	Clique	157,709	502,966
z	MathOverflow [23]	User answers or comments on questions on MathOverflow	Social	Clique	24,506	198,040
A	StackOverflow [23]	User answers or comments on questions on StackOverflow	Social	Clique	38,379	618,519

(continued)

Table 2 (continued)

	Name	Description	Type	Structure	Nodes	Edges
B	SuperUser [23]	User answers or comments on questions on SuperUser	Social	Clique	124,528	541,466
C	UCLA AS [3]	UCLA AS level internet topology	Computer	Individual	38,055	224,545
D	US Air Traffic [23]	Flights among all commercial airports in the US	Transport	Individual	623	14,952
E	Wiki Talk [23]	Wikipedia users editing each other's Talk page	Social	Individual	116,661	329,805

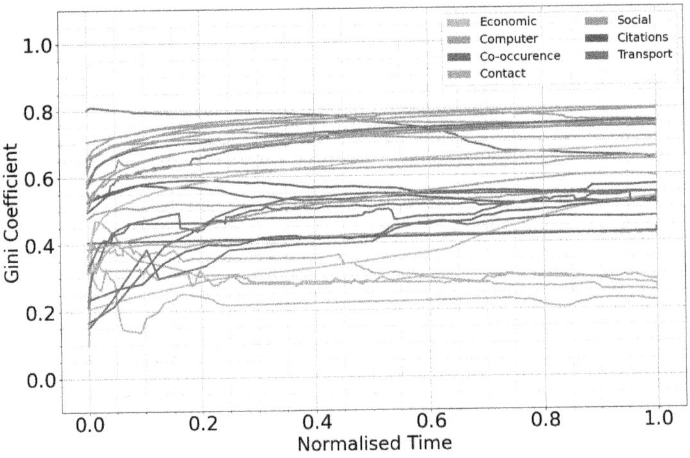

Fig. 1 Equality of data set corpus networks coloured by data type over normalised time, where all network lifetimes are normalised to the range 0 to 1

The contact networks are collected by measuring contact between people in physical space. Therefore the degree of a node is limited by the number of people that can be physically present in the space during the measurement interval. These limitations on network evolution would suggest a more equal distribution of degree as it is more likely that two individuals will spend time together than a less constrained system. Online social networks do not have this physical limitation. For example, if an individual is not interested in the software language Python, then they will not interact with the Python section of stackoverflow.com. This means there is less chance of densification as the interactions are less likely to occur than a physical contact network.

5.2 *Mobility Taxonomy*

To look at how the mobility taxonomy varies with time for every data set network we chose values of t_1 evenly spaced as the network grows. To achieve this we pick values of t_1 corresponding to $10, 20, \ldots, 90\%$ of the final number of edges being present and t_2 corresponding to all edges being present.

5.2.1 Taxonomy Aspect Evolution

These values of the mobility taxonomy were plotted against time to show how they individually evolve with time in Fig. 2. The data set types are again used to differentiate the networks, and it can be seen that most of the networks have a similar evolution for each of the aspects. However there are notable exceptions in each case.

Mobility and neighbourhood mobility positively correlate with a coefficient of 0.79 at 10% of edges, which can be seen in the vast majority of networks reaching high levels of correlation for both aspects. Positive correlation coefficients for these aspects signify a more static hierarchy of degree in the network over time (i.e individual nodes rarely change their place in the degree hierarchy). As static degree hierarchies are sometimes thought of as a given in real world network degree, it is unexpected we found limited evidence of networks which have a somewhat mobile degree hierarchy.

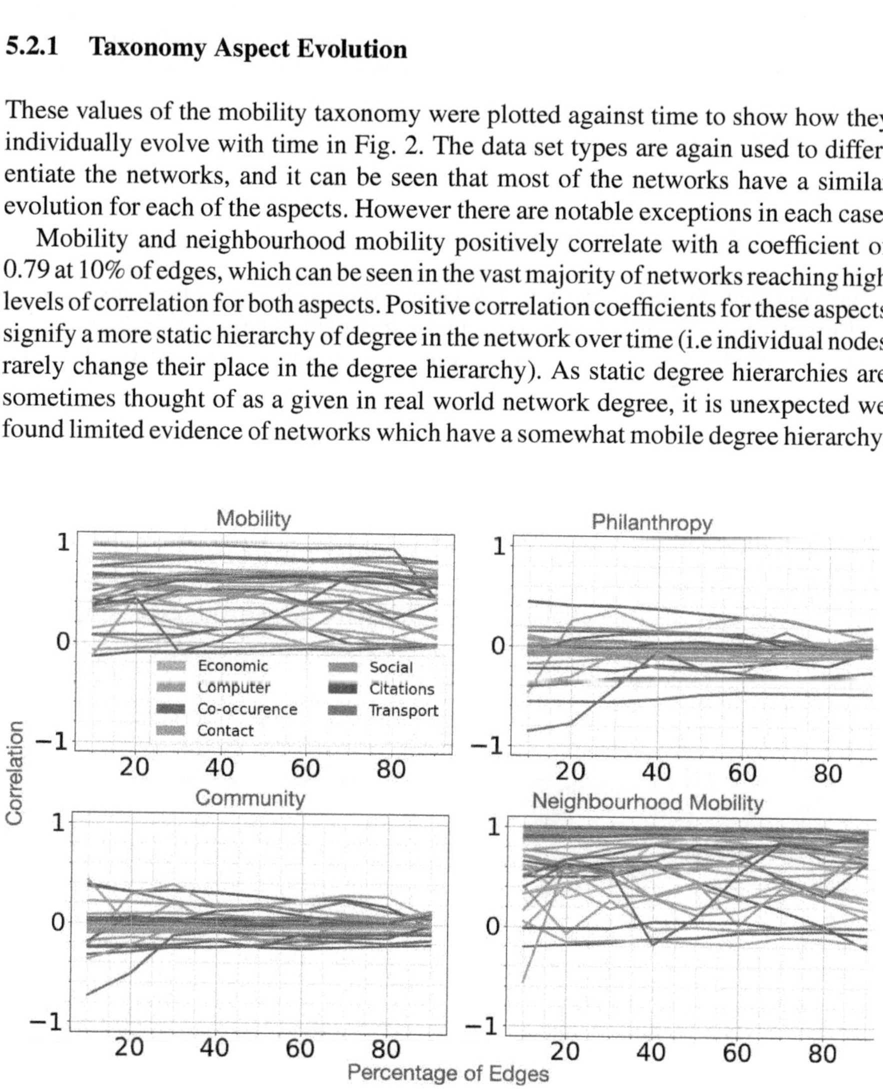

Fig. 2 Every data set corpus network for each aspect of the mobility taxonomy coloured by data type. The x-axis represents t_1 characterised as percentage of life of the network. The y-axis shows the correlation coefficient as measured using Pearson correlation

However, this is largely in contact networks where, perhaps the large degree nodes happened to have many contacts at one time and getting the mobile degree hierarchy is merely regression to the mean.

The aspects community and philanthropy have a Pearson correlation of 0.48 at 10% of edges. Some networks are positive or negative in both but most of the networks show very little either way. For those on the periphery, there is a noticeable trend towards zero for both positive and negative correlations suggesting a longer time in the network correlates with a more significant influence from these aspects. Negative values of philanthropy can be thought of as nodes that grow themselves but have a detrimental effect on the growth of their neighbours. This is largely seen in co-occurrence networks and we might think of a "prima-donna" effect where characters that gain attention drain attention from their co-stars.

5.2.2 Principal Component Analysis

To take the analysis further we correlated each aspect with each other, plus the Gini coefficient results at time t_1 for completeness, e.g all of the data set results for mobility with those of philanthropy. This resulted in a seven-dimensional matrix which we reduce to its two highest variance components using Principal Component Analysis for visualisation.

Having time dependent values for the PCA means we are able to show how the networks evolve in time. These results are plotted in Fig. 3 with the data and structural types from Table 2 highlighted using colours and shapes. One striking feature is that many network are clustered together in the upper left quadrant of the graph. These networks are also much less prone to large changes in position, i.e they are more ossified, than those on the periphery of the cluster. A slight trend occurs in how the

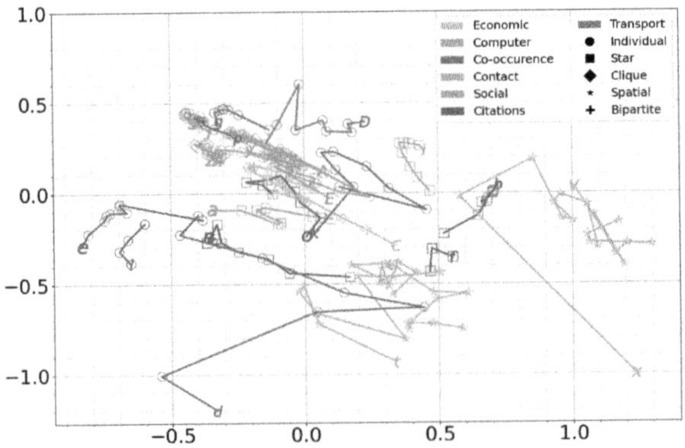

Fig. 3 Principal component analysis of the mobility taxonomy, including equality, with each data set marked by its associated letter (see Table 2) on its first time-step. The plotted lines denote the data sets through 9 time-steps, each step plotted with a shape corresponding to its structure and the colour corresponding to its type

further the network is from the origin the more volatile its position on the PCA is over time. This volatility of position also correlates with a fewer number of nodes in the networks, i.e smaller networks have more changeability in their taxonomy aspects over time.

6 Conclusions

In this paper we have shown how tracking the statistics of individual nodes and their neighbours, specifically the degree centrality, throughout the lifetime of the network can bring structural and developmental insight into the network's evolution. Each of the mobility taxonomy aspects, along with equality, show different mechanisms underlying the evolution of a network and combining knowledge gained from each of them draws a vivid picture of how individual nodes interact with each other.

Also, running a PCA on the whole mobility taxonomy (plus equality) was shown to distinguish between networks into somewhat distinct categories. The time evolving PCA allowed for determination of network ossification and it was found that social networks are more likely to be ossified whereas co-occurrence and contact networks are less likely, though network size is also a contributing factor.

The techniques outlined in this paper are of great use for analysing trends of nodes in networks which evolve with time. Our main focus for future expansion is to delve deeply into the inter-node interaction dynamics of a single network and build understanding of causation for network-level phenomena from individual node interactions.

Acknowledgements The authors wish to acknowledge the support of Moogsoft Ltd. for funding this research.

References

1. Barabási, A.L., Albert, R.: Emergence of scaling in random networks. Science **286**(5439), 509–512 (1999). https://doi.org/10.1126/science.286.5439.509
2. Breen, R.: Social Mobility in Europe. OUP Oxford (2004)
3. Clegg, R.G., et al.: Measuring the likelihood of models for network evolution. In: Proceedings of INFOCOM'09, pp. 272–277 (2009)
4. Corman, S.R., Kuhn, T., Mcphee, R.D.: Studying complex discursive systems. Hum. Commun. Res. (2002). https://doi.org/10.1111/j.1468-2958.2002.tb00802.x
5. Dimaggio, P., Garip, F.: Network effects and social inequality. Annu. Rev. Sociol. **38**, 93–118 (2012). https://doi.org/10.1146/annurev.soc.012809.102545
6. Erikson, R., Goldthorpe, J.H.: The Constant Flux: A Study of Class Mobility in Industrial Societies. Oxford University Press (1992)
7. Fire, M., Guestrin, C.: The rise and fall of network stars. Inf. Process. Manag. **57**(2) (2020). https://doi.org/10.1016/j.ipm.2019.05.002
8. Fortunato, S., et al.: Scale-free network growth by ranking. Phys. Rev. Lett. **96**(21), 1–4 (2006). https://doi.org/10.1103/PhysRevLett.96.218701

9. Fowler, J.H., et al.: Network analysis and the law. Polit. Anal. **15**(3), 324–346 (2007). https://doi.org/10.1093/pan/mpm011
10. Génois, M., et al.: Data on face-to-face contacts in an office building suggest a low-cost vaccination strategy based on community linkers. Netw. Sci. **3**(3), 326–347 (2015). https://doi.org/10.1017/nws.2015.10
11. Gini, C.: Variabilità e mutabilità. Memorie di metodologica statistica (1912)
12. Granovetter, M.S.: The strength of weak ties. Am. J. Sociol. **78**(6), 1360–1380 (1973)
13. Hall, B.H., et al: The NBER Patent Citation Data File: Lessons, Insights and Methodological Tools. NBER Cambridge, Mass (2001). https://doi.org/10.3386/w8498
14. Holanda, A.J., et al: Character networks and book genre classification. IJMPC **30**(8) (2019). https://doi.org/10.1142/S012918311950058X
15. Iñiguez, G., Pineda, C., Gershenson, C., Barabási, A.L.: Universal dynamics of ranking. Nat. Commun. (2021). http://arxiv.org/abs/2104.13439
16. Isella, L., et al.: What's in a crowd? analysis of face-to-face behavioral networks. JTB **271**(1), 166–180 (2011). https://doi.org/10.1016/j.jtbi.2010.11.033
17. Kumar, S., et al: Community interaction and conflict on the web. In: Proceedings of the 2018 World Wide Web Conference, pp. 933–943 (2018). https://doi.org/10.1145/3178876.3186141
18. Lim, E.P., et al.: Detecting product review spammers using rating behaviors. In: Proceedings of the 19th ACM International Conference on Information and Knowledge Management, pp. 939–948 (2010)
19. Lorenz, M.O.: Methods of measuring the concentration of wealth. Publ. Am. Stat. Assoc. **9**(70), 209–219 (1905)
20. Mayer, S.E., Lopoo, L.M.: Has the intergenerational transmission of economic status changed? JHR **40**(1), 169–185 (2005). https://doi.org/10.3368/jhr.xl.1.169
21. Nsour, F., Sayama, H.: Hot-get-richer network growth model. In: International Conference on Complex Networks and Their Applications, pp. 532–543. Springer, Berlin (2020)
22. Panzarasa, P., et al.: Patterns and dynamics of users' behavior and interaction: network analysis of an online community. J. Am. Soc. Inf. Sci. Technol. **60**(5), 911–932 (2009)
23. Paranjape, A., et al: Motifs in temporal networks. In: Proceedings of the tenth ACM International Conference on Web Search and Data Mining, pp. 601–610 (2017). https://doi.org/10.1145/3018661.3018731
24. Park, D., et al: Novelty and influence of creative works, and quantifying patterns of advances based on probabilistic references networks. EPJ Data Sci. **9**(1) (2020). https://doi.org/10.1140/epjds/s13688-019-0214-8
25. Redner, S.: Citation statistics from 110 years of physical review. Phys. Today **58**(6), 49–54 (2005). https://doi.org/10.1063/1.1996475
26. Solon, G.: Intergenerational Income Mobility in the United States. The American Economic Review, pp. 393–408 (1992)
27. Stehlé, J., et al: High-resolution measurements of face-to-face contact patterns in a primary school. PLoS One **6**(8) (2011). https://doi.org/10.1371/journal.pone.0023176
28. Szreter, S.R.S.: The genesis of the registrar-general's social classification of occupations. Br. J. Sociol. **35**(4), 522–546 (1984)
29. Taylor, D., et al.: Eigenvector-based centrality measures for temporal networks. MMS **15**(1), 537–574 (2017). https://doi.org/10.1137/16M1066142
30. Valverde, S., Sole, R.V.: Punctuated equilibrium in the large-scale evolution of programming languages. JRSI **12**(107) (2015). https://doi.org/10.1098/rsif.2015.0249
31. Vanhems, P., et al: Estimating potential infection transmission routes in hospital wards using wearable proximity sensors. PloS One **8**(9) (2013). https://doi.org/10.1371/journal.pone.0073970
32. Viswanath, B., et al.: On the evolution of user interaction in facebook. In: Proceedings of the 2nd ACM Workshop on Online Social Networks, pp. 37–42 (2009)
33. Wachs, J., et al.: Corruption risk in contracting markets. IJDSA **12**(1), 45–60 (2021). https://doi.org/10.1007/s41060-019-00204-1
34. Zhou, B., Lu, X., Holme, P.: Universal evolution patterns of degree assortativity in social networks. Soc. Netw. **63**, 47–55 (2020). https://doi.org/10.1016/j.socnet.2020.04.004

Broadcast Graphs with Nodes of Limited Memory

Saber Gholami and Hovhannes A. Harutyunyan

Abstract Broadcasting is the process of information dissemination in a network in which a sender, called the *originator*, wishes to inform all network members as promptly as possible. The broadcast time of a vertex is the minimum time needed to inform all vertices of the network, while the broadcast time of the graph is the maximum broadcast time to broadcast from any originator. A *broadcast graph (bg)* is a graph with minimum possible broadcast time from any originator. Additionally, a *minimum broadcast graph (mbg)* is a *bg* with the minimum possible number of edges. In classical broadcasting, an omniscient who is equipped with adequate memory knows the situation of the whole network as well as the originator in every unit of time. Considering the growth in today's networks, this is either idealistic in some contexts (such as physical circuits) or at least costly in others (such as telecommunication networks). Consequently, different variations of broadcasting have been suggested in the literature. In this study, we focus on comparing two branches of broadcasting, namely the universal list and messy broadcasting models. To this aim, we propose several general upper bounds for the universal lists by comparing it with the messy broadcasting model. Besides, we propose *mbg*'s on n vertices for $n \leq 10$ and sparse *bg*'s for $11 \leq n \leq 14$ under universal list model. Afterward, we introduce the first infinite families of *bg*'s under the universal lists model. Lastly, we prove that hypercubes are *mbg* under the universal lists.

1 Introduction

High-performance interconnection networks connect compute nodes on a cluster computer so that they can communicate with each other. A cluster computer comprises multiple compute nodes, each having several processing elements. The design

S. Gholami (✉) · H. A. Harutyunyan
Department of Computer Science and Software Engineering, Concordia University, Montreal, QC H3G 1M8, Canada
e-mail: m_olamin@cs.concordia.ca

H. A. Harutyunyan
e-mail: haruty@cs.concordia.ca

D. Pacheco et al. (eds.), *Complex Networks XIII*, Springer Proceedings in Complexity,
https://doi.org/10.1007/978-3-031-17658-6_3

of such networks is decisive, specifically in High-Performance Computing (HPC) systems. Moreover, an interconnection network is utilized whenever synchronization among the processing elements or exchange of intermediate results is required. More importantly, the overall network performance and the entire system are determined by the interconnection network topology and the routing scheme [2]. In particular, low latency, high bandwidth, and memory-efficient communication between the compute nodes are necessary for HPC applications to scale appropriately on multiple machines. Therefore, studying interconnection networks and, specifically, the algorithms that move the data around the processing units are pivotal in the performance of such applications [32], particularly with limited memory. A vital problem in the area of information dissemination is *broadcasting* which refers to the process of distributing a piece of information in a communication network. In particular, a message held initially by a single network member must be promptly transmitted to all network members. This is achieved by placing a series of calls over the network's communication links while respecting the following limitations: A call involves precisely two network members and is executed in a single unit of time. Although a node can only pass the message to one of its neighbors at a time, a vertex may receive the message from multiple senders at each time unit.

A network is modeled by an undirected graph $G = (V, E)$, where V is a set of vertices representing the network members, and E is a set of bidirectional communication links between the members of the network. It is generally assumed that G is a connected graph. The broadcast time of a vertex $v \in V(G)$ under the classical model is denoted by $B_{cl}(v, G)$ and is defined to be the minimum number of time units required for a message to be transmitted to all members of V, originating from v. By definition, the broadcast time of the graph G under the classical model is the maximum broadcast time of any vertex v in G, and it is denoted by $B_{cl}(G)$: $B_{cl}(G) = \max\{B_{cl}(v, G)|v \in V(G)\}$. Not only it is NP-Hard to find $B_{cl}(G)$ and $B_{cl}(v, G)$ for arbitrary graphs and originators [28], it is proved that this problem remains NP-Hard in more restricted families of networks [7, 23]. Therefore, several models of broadcasting are defined in the literature, such as the universal lists model and messy broadcasting, in which some constraints of the classical model are relaxed.

This paper discusses the definitions and the related works in Sect. 2. Then we study the relation between two branches of the broadcasting problem in Sect. 3. We also propose several graphs for the universal list model for which broadcasting could be finished as quickly as theoretically possible from any originator in Sect. 4. Additionally, we prove that a hypercube H_d is a graph with minimum possible edges for any value of 2^k to achieve the minimum broadcast time. Section 5 concludes this paper.

2 Background and Literature Review

2.1 Classical Broadcasting

The broadcast scheme[1] of the classical model is the series of calls that are placed in the network. This could be interpreted as an ordering of the neighbors of each vertex [6]. Consider vertex u as the originator. Once a vertex v receives the source message, it will utilize its list, denoted by l_v^u, and pass the information to its uninformed neighbors following the order of its list. A valid broadcast scheme contains the lists such that having placed all calls, every member of the network is equipped with the message. However, the vital issue with the classical model is that those lists differ for various originators. Therefore, each vertex must maintain several lists depending on the originator and adapt its behavior accordingly. In particular, a vertex v has to maintain up to $|V|$ different lists, denoted by $l_v^u, \forall u \in V(G)$. Indeed, this is not efficient in terms of memory usage.

The problem of broadcasting under the classical model is well studied in the literature. The general direction to follow is to either propose an optimal, or near-optimal, broadcast scheme for a specific family of networks [13, 14, 19, 35], or to come up with a heuristic or approximation algorithm [9, 12, 20, 27, 31]. For surveys on broadcasting and related problems we refer to [11, 18, 21, 22].

2.2 Broadcasting with Universal List

To handle the above-mentioned drawbacks, another variant of broadcasting is introduced [6, 33]. Suppose every vertex of the network is given a universal list, and it has to follow the list, regardless of the originator. So, when a vertex v receives the message, it should transmit the message to its neighbors following the ordering given in its list l_v. In this model, we drop the superscript in the notation of l_v as the list is universal for all originators. There are three sub-models defined using universal lists:

1. *Non-adaptive*: Once a vertex v receives the message; it will re-transmit it to all the vertices on l_v, even if v has received it from that particular vertex. The broadcast time of a graph G following this model is denoted by $B_{na}(G)$.
2. *Adaptive*: Once informed, a vertex v will send the message to its neighbors according to l_v, but it will skip the neighbors from which it has received the message. The broadcast time of a graph G following this model is denoted by $B_a(G)$.
3. *Fully-adaptive*: Once a vertex v is informed, it will follow its list and pass the message to the first vertex on l_v, which is not already informed. In other words, not only does the sender, v, skip all those neighbors that it received the message

[1] Or broadcast algorithm.

from, but it will also skip all other informed vertices. The broadcast time of a graph G following this model is denoted by $B_{fa}(G)$.

It is obvious that for an arbitrary graph G, $B_{cl}(G) \leq B_{fa}(G) \leq B_a(G) \leq B_{na}(G)$ [15]. Considering graph $G = (V, E)$ in which $|V| = n$, a broadcast scheme for non-adaptive, adaptive, or fully-adaptive model can be viewed as a matrix $\sigma_{n\times\Delta}$, where row i of σ corresponds to an ordering of the neighbors of vertex v_i. Assuming this vertex has degree d_i, the cells $\sigma_{[i][d_i+1]}, \sigma_{[i][d_i+2]}, \ldots, \sigma_{[i][\Delta]}$ will be NULL. By definition: $\Delta = \max\{d_i : 1 \leq i \leq n\}$. We denote all possible schemes by Σ. Let M be one of the three models using universal lists ($M \in \{na, a, fa\}$) and fix a graph G. For any broadcast scheme $\sigma \in \Sigma$, we denote by $B^{\sigma}_M(v, G)$ the time steps needed to inform all the vertices in G from the source v while following the scheme σ under model M. Moreover, the broadcast time of a graph G under model M with scheme σ, $B^{\sigma}_M(G)$, is defined as the maximum $B^{\sigma}_M(v, G)$ over all possible originators $v \in V(G)$. Lastly, $B_M(G)$ is the minimum $B^{\sigma}_M(G)$ over all possible schemes $\sigma \in \Sigma$:

$$\begin{aligned} B^{\sigma}_M(G) &= \max_{v\in V}\{B^{\sigma}_M(v, G)\} \\ B_M(G) &= \min_{\sigma\in\Sigma}\{B^{\sigma}_M(G)\} \end{aligned} \tag{1}$$

Broadcasting with the universal list was firstly introduced by Slater et al. indirectly [35] as they proved that for any tree T, $B_{cl}(T) = B_a(T)$. Afterward, the formal definition for this sub-model was presented in [33] alongside the optimal broadcast scheme for trees under the adaptive model. Also, Diks and Pelc [6] distinguished between the adaptive and non-adaptive models while proposing optimal broadcast schemes for several families of networks. We must also refer to [15, 17, 25] as the most notable researches in this area.

2.3 Messy Broadcasting

This model, introduced in [1], is similar to the universal list model, but the network nodes have even more limited memory. In messy broadcasting, every informed vertex randomly chooses a neighbor and sends the message. Thus, in this model, the goal is to study the worst behavior of the network members. There are three sub-models defined for messy broadcasting:

1. *Model* M_1: Each vertex knows the state of its neighbors, informed or uninformed. Therefore, once a vertex gets informed, it only has to send the message to its uninformed neighbors in some arbitrary order.
2. *Model* M_2: Each vertex knows from which vertices it has received the message and considers those as informed vertices. Thus, once vertex v gets informed, it will randomly send the message to the neighbors who have not sent it to v before.
3. *Model* M_3: Each vertex only knows to which vertices it has sent the message and will consider them as informed neighbors, all other neighbours are considered as

uninformed for this vertex. Therefore, a vertex will send the message to all of its neighbors in an arbitrary order once it gets informed.

The broadcast time of a vertex v under model M_i is denoted by $t_i(v)$, for $i = 1, 2, 3$, and it is defined to be the *maximum* number of time units required to complete broadcasting originating from vertex v over all possible broadcast schemes. Also, the broadcast time of the graph G under model M_i is denoted by $t_i(G)$, for $i = 1, 2, 3$, and is the maximum broadcast time of any vertex v of G.

The exact value of $t_i(G)$ for complete graphs, paths, cycles, and complete d-ary trees are known for $i = 1, 2, 3$ [16]. Also, in [5] multidimensional directed tori and complete bipartite graphs are studied. Moreover, the average-case messy broadcasting time of various networks such as stars, paths, cycles, complete d-ary trees and hypercubes are studied in [29].

In summary, the differences among these three broadcasting models are as follows: In the classical model, being the quickest among all, there exists an omniscient who knows the network's exact situation at every single unit of time. Therefore, it will guide network members to broadcast as efficiently as possible while adapting their behavior according to the originator. This omniscient may be considered as a network manager who is provided with sufficient memory for each node and allows them to change their behavior depending on the originator. In the universal list model, however, the network manager cannot behave as prodigal as the previous model since the memory is limited regarding each member. Therefore, the behavior of all members, a.k.a, the universal lists, are to be set beforehand, and then, the broadcasting will be performed according to the lists. Indeed, the network manager tries to minimize the broadcast time of the network as much as possible. In contrast, in messy broadcasting, there is no one monitoring the situation of the network, and the members will act randomly. Hence, the worst behavior of the network with respect to the broadcast time is of interest.

3 Comparison of Universal List and Messy Broadcasting

We start with a primary result:

Lemma 1 *For any graph G:*
$B_{fa}(G) \leq t_1(G)$.
$B_a(G) \leq t_2(G)$.
$B_{na}(G) \leq t_3(G)$.

Proof We begin by proving the first statement. For graph G, consider an arbitrary broadcast scheme σ under the fully-adaptive model. Fix the originator u, and then, start broadcasting from u using σ. Once performing the broadcasting, if a vertex v skips v' on its list at time t, it means that vertex v' was informed by time unit $t - 1$. Now we may use the same scheme σ for broadcasting under model M_1. Note that any vertex such as v will skip its neighbour v' at time t since v' must have been informed at any time $t' < t$ following σ.

In other words, assume that the broadcast time of graph G under the fully-adaptive model using σ is denoted by $B^{\sigma}_{fa}(G)$. Note that the value of $B^{\sigma}_{fa}(G)$ is a lower bound on $t_1(G)$, since $t_1(G)$ is the maximum value among all possible broadcast schemes. Thus, $B^{\sigma}_{fa}(G) \leq t_1(G)$. Since $B_{fa}(G) \leq B^{\sigma}_{fa}(G)$, the result follows.

The proofs of the second and the third statements go in the same direction. To illustrate, the value realized by following an arbitrary broadcast scheme σ under the adaptive model is always a valid candidate for model M_2: $B_a(G) \leq B^{\sigma}_a(G) \leq t_2(G)$. Observe that the nature of the vertices that are to be skipped under the adaptive model is the same as that of model M_2. The same is also true for the non-adaptive model and messy model M_3: $B_{na}(G) \leq B^{\sigma}_{na}(G) \leq t_3(G)$. □

We will also give some graphs for which the inequalities of Lemma 1 are on their boundaries. For the equality, consider path P_n on n vertices. It is proved in [15] that $B_{fa}(P_n) = B_a(P_n) = n - 1$. Also, from [16] we know that $t_1(P_n) = t_2(P_n) = n - 1$. Also, consider Star S_n for non-adaptive model where $B_{na}(S_n) = n$ [6]. The same value is achieved under model $M_3 : t_3(S_n) = n$. This shows that the upper bounds of Lemma 1 cannot be improved in general. Besides, one may suspect that the values of Lemma 1 are always equal. As a counter example, consider complete graph K_n on n vertices. From [16] one may notice that $t_1(K_n) = t_2(K_n) = t_3(K_n) = n - 1$. However, a non-trivial upper bound presented in [6] suggests that $B_{fa}(K_n) \leq B_a(K_n) \leq B_{na}(K_n) \leq \lceil \log n \rceil + 2\lceil \sqrt{\log n} \rceil$. Additionally, we argue that there is no relation between model M_2 and non-adaptive model, or between model M_1 and the adaptive model. As an example regarding the first case, consider Path P_n and the Complete graph K_n for which: $B_{na}(K_n) \leq \lceil \log n \rceil + 2\lceil \sqrt{\log n} \rceil < n - 1 = t_2(K_n)$ and $B_{na}(P_n) = \lceil \frac{3n}{2} \rceil - 2 > n - 1 = t_2(P_n)$ [6]. We also conjecture that the same is true for the second case, though we are not able to find a simple graph G with $B_a(G) > t_1(G)$.

Using Lemma 1, several upper bounds on $B_M(G)$ for $M \in \{fa, a, na\}$ could be achieved for any connected graph G with n vertices and m edges, diameter $d(G)$, and the maximum degree of Δ:

Corollary 1 $B_{na}(G) \leq 2m - 1$, *and* $B_{fa}(G) \leq B_a(G) \leq m$.

Corollary 2 $B_{na}(G) \leq d(G) \cdot \Delta$, *and* $B_{fa}(G) \leq B_a(G) \leq d(G) \cdot (\Delta - 1) + 1$.

The truth of Corollary 1 can be realized by noticing that an edge could be used at most twice under the non-adaptive model, once in each direction. However, once the last vertex is informed, the process will stop, and it will not call back using the same edge. For the fully-adaptive and adaptive model, on the other hand, an edge (u, v) may be utilized at most once, either for sending from u to v or vice versa. The result follows. Besides, the truth of Corollary 2 could be realized by utilizing Corollary 2.1 of [16] which proves the same inequality on $t_i(G)$ for $i = 1, 2, 3$.

4 Broadcast Graphs Under the Fully-Adaptive Model

A *broadcast graph (bg)* is a graph $G = (V, E)$ in which broadcasting could be completed within the minimum possible time starting from any originator. In classical model, the minimum possible time is $\lceil \log n \rceil$ for a graph on n vertices, thus, for an arbitrary broadcast graph G: $\forall u \in V(G) : B_{cl}(u, G) = \lceil \log n \rceil$. Additionally, a *minimum broadcast graph (mbg)* is the *bg* with the minimum possible number of edges. We denote by $B^{(M)}(n)$ the broadcast function for an arbitrary value of n under model $M \in \{cl, fa\}$, which is the number of edges associated with the mbg for n. Finding mbg's for different values of n is quite vital since they represent the networks with minimum cost in which broadcasting could be performed as quickly as possible from any originator.

Although this problem is well studied under $M = cl$ for several values of n, there is no comparative study under universal lists models. Despite the considerable effort, an *mbg* is known only for very few n under the classical model. In particular, Hypercubes H_k [10] and Knodel graphs $W_{k,2^k}$ [21, 26] are mbg's for $n = 2^k$, while the latter family is also an mbg for $n = 2^k - 2$ [8, 24]. The value of $B^{(cl)}(n)$ is also known for small values of $n \leq 32$ except for $n = 23, 24, 25$ [3, 4, 10, 30, 34].

4.1 *mbg's for Some Values of n* ≤ 16

In what follows, the mbg's under the fully-adaptive model for all values of $n \leq 10$ are presented. Moreover, we provide upper bounds on the value of $B^{(fa)}(n)$ for $11 \leq n \leq 14$. We first prove a lower bound on the value of $B^{(fa)}(n)$:

Lemma 2 *If there is a graph G on n vertices for which $B_{fa}(G) = \lceil \log n \rceil$, then $B^{(cl)}(n) \leq B^{(fa)}(n)$.*

Proof Consider an arbitrary graph G_1 with n_1 vertices and m_1 edges under fully-adaptive model such that $B_{fa}(G_1) = \lceil \log n_1 \rceil$. Then, G_1 is a broadcast graph. Observe that for any graph G with n vertices, $\lceil \log n \rceil \leq B_{cl}(G) \leq B_{fa}(G)$ [15]. Therefore, $B_{cl}(G_1) = \lceil \log n_1 \rceil$, and G_1 is a broadcast graph under classical model as well. Thus, m_1 is an upper bound for $B^{cl}(n_1)$. The result follows. □

Recall that the broadcast time of a Cycle C_n under the fully-adaptive model is $\lceil \frac{n}{2} \rceil$ [15]. This value is as low as $\lceil \log n \rceil$ for $n \leq 6$. Consequently, since C_n is also an mbg under the classical model and due to Lemma 2, the following corollary is concluded:

Corollary 3 *Cycle C_n is mbg under the fully-adaptive model for* $4 \leq n \leq 6$.

Hereafter, we will prove that the mbg's for classical broadcasting, presented in [10], are also mbg's for the fully-adaptive model for $n = 7, 9$, and 10. Figure 1a–c illustrate the mbg's for these values under the fully-adaptive model which are identical to that of classical model. The broadcast schemes for these graphs are presented

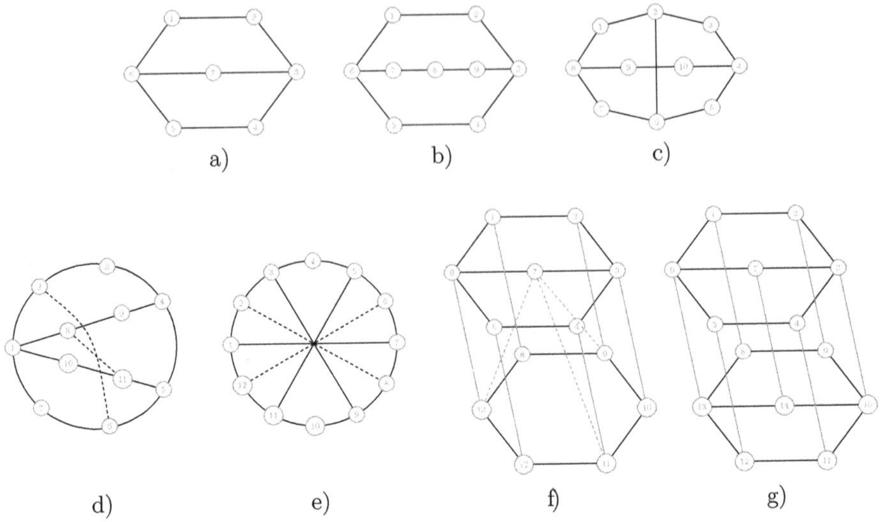

Fig. 1 **a–c** *mbg*'s on 7, 9, and 10 vertices under the fully-adaptive model. **d–g** *bg*'s on 11, 12, 13 and 14 vertices under the fully-adaptive model

Table 1 The known values of $B^{(fa)}(n)$ for $n < 15$

n	3	4	5	6	7	8	9	10	11	12	13	14
Lower bound on $B^{(fa)}(n)$	2	4	5	6	8	12	10	12	13	15	18	21
Upper bound on $B^{(fa)}(n)$	2	4	5	6	8	12	10	12	15	17	23	23

in the Appendix. This problem becomes more difficult for $n \geq 11$ under the fully-adaptive model. For instance, our exhaustive search on more than 4000 broadcast schemes on *mbg*'s with $n = 11, \ldots, 15$ vertices did not result in a broadcast scheme that achieves $B^{\sigma}_{fa}(G) = 4$. However, by adding a few more edges to the *mbg*'s on the classical model, an upper bound on the value of $B^{(fa)}(n)$ is obtained for $11 \leq n \leq 14$. These *bg*'s are presented in Fig. 1d–g, respectively, while the broadcast schemes achieving time 4 are presented in the Appendix. Table 1 summarizes the results of this section.

4.2 *General Construction of bg's*

In what follows, we present a general construction for creating the first infinite families of broadcast graphs under the fully-adaptive model for $n = 6 \times 2^k, 7 \times 2^k, 9 \times 2^k$, and 10×2^k.

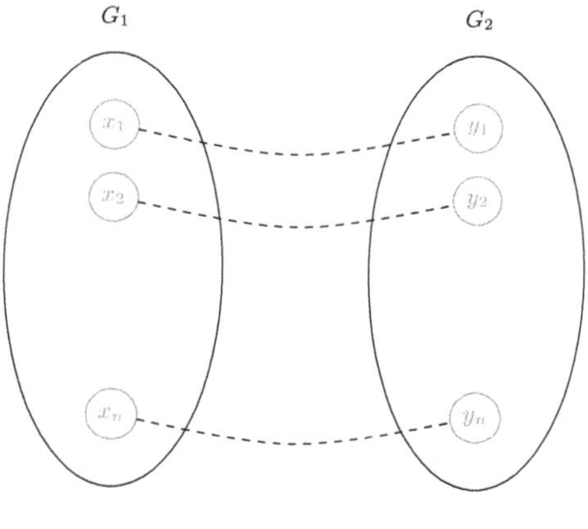

Fig. 2 Construction of graph G'

Lemma 3 *Consider a graph $G = (V, E)$ with n vertices, m edges, and $B_{fa}(G) = \tau$. It is always possible to construct a graph $G' = (V', E')$ with $2n$ vertices, $2m + n$ edges, and $B_{fa}(G') = \tau + 1$.*

Proof First, make two copies of G and denote them by $G_1 = (V_1, E_1)$ and $G_2 = (V_2, E_2)$. Also, assume that $|V_1| = |V_2| = n$, and $|E_1| = |E_2| = m$. Let $V_1 = \{x_1, x_2, \ldots, x_n\}$ and $V_2 = \{y_1, y_2, \ldots, y_n\}$, where y_i is the image of x_i; $i = 1, \ldots, n$. The vertices of G' consist of the union of those graphs: $V' = V_1 \cup V_2$. Also, the edges of G' comprise of the set of edges of G_1 and G_2 as well as n additional inter-layer edges: $E' = E_1 \cup E_2 \cup E_{\text{inter}}$, such that: $E_{\text{inter}} = \{(x_i, y_i) | \forall i : 1 \leq i \leq n\}$. Figure 2 portrays this construction.

Denote the broadcast scheme of graph G under fully-adaptive model by σ such that $B^{\sigma}_{fa}(G) = \tau$. We are interested in making a broadcast scheme σ' for G' in a way that $B^{\sigma'}_{fa}(G') = \tau + 1$. The vertices of G' will preserve their broadcast scheme in G and append their corresponding vertex as the last vertex on their ordering. In other words, the ordering of vertex x_i, $1 \leq i \leq n$ is as follows: $x_i :<$ within $G_1, y_i >$. Similarly, $\forall i; 1 \leq i \leq n : y_i :<$ within $G_2, x_i >$. These orderings imply that once a vertex gets informed, it will follow the broadcasting within its subgraph, either G_1 or G_2, and on its last call, it will inform its corresponding vertex. Suppose vertex u is the originator in graph G' which is located in partition $p \in \{1, 2\}$. Broadcasting from originator u in G' under fully-adaptive model could be done in two phases:

- *Phase 1*: During the first τ time units, all vertices in partition p will be informed following σ' since each vertex will follow the same procedure as it had to follow within the smaller sub-graph G_p.
- *Phase 2*: At time $\tau + 1$ every vertex of partition p will make a call to their corresponding vertex in the other partition, simultaneously.

Note that a vertex can finish its first phase sooner than time τ and send the message to its corresponding vertex at a time $t' < \tau$. However, this will not slow down the broadcasting process. Therefore, $B^{\sigma'}_{fa}(G') = \tau + 1$. □

We will use the following notation for expressing the result of Lemma 3:

Theorem 1 $(G, n, m, \tau) \rightarrow (G', 2n, 2m + n, \tau + 1)$.

In which the arguments are the graph, the number of vertices, the number of edges, and the broadcast time of the graph under the fully adaptive model, respectively. Thereafter, using Theorem 1, we will argue the following corollaries:

Corollary 4 *For any positive* $k : (G, n, m, \tau) \rightarrow (G', 2^k n, 2^k m + k2^{k-1} n, \tau + k)$.

Proof The truth of this Corollary could be realized by repeating the procedure of Theorem 1 for k times. Observe that the number of vertices doubles each time. Also, the number of edges by repeating this procedure for k times, m_k, could be understood by solving the following recursion: $m_k = 2m_{k-1} + n_{k-1}$, in which m_{k-1} refers to the number of edges by applying the construction for $k - 1$ times, and n_{k-1} denotes the number of nodes by applying the construction for $k - 1$ times. The base case of this recursion is $m_0 = m$ and $n_0 = n$. □

Corollary 5 *For any positive* k, $(G, n, m, \lceil \log n \rceil) \rightarrow (G', 2^k n, 2^k m + k2^{k-1} n, \lceil \log n \rceil + k)$.

Proof This could be realized by replacing τ with $\lceil \log n \rceil$ in Corollary 4. Note that using this construction for a broadcast graph G on n vertices, the obtained graph G' remains a *bg* on $n \cdot 2^k$ vertices. □

An upper bound for the number of edges of a graph on $2^k n$ vertices could be realized by considering a complete graph on $2^k n$ vertices which has $\frac{2^k n \times (2^k n - 1)}{2} = 2^{k-1}(2n^2 - n)$ vertices. However, the graph G' presented in Corollary 5 has $2^{k-1}(2m + kn)$ vertices. Therefore, for infinitely large values of n, as long as $m \in o(n^2)$, the construction for the graph G' will create a sufficiently sparse graph compared to the complete graph. This makes this construction efficient in terms of the cost associated with creating edges for a fixed value of n. Using Corollary 5, we will introduce some broadcast graphs for several values of n.

Proposition 1 *For any positive k:*
$(G, 6, 6, 3) \rightarrow (G', 6 \cdot 2^k, 6 \cdot 2^k + 6k2^{k-1}, 3 + k)$,
$(G, 7, 8, 3) \rightarrow (G', 7 \cdot 2^k, 8 \cdot 2^k + 7k2^{k-1}, 3 + k)$,
$(G, 9, 10, 4) \rightarrow (G', 9 \cdot 2^k, 10 \cdot 2^k + 9k2^{k-1}, 4 + k)$,
$(G, 10, 12, 4) \rightarrow (G', 10 \cdot 2^k, 12 \cdot 2^k + 10k2^{k-1}, 4 + k)$.

Proof The proof of this Proposition directly follows from Corollary 5 and *mbg*'s on $n = 6, 7, 9$, and 10 vertices presented in Sect. 4.1. □

The following Theorem summarizes the presented results:

Theorem 2 *For any integer* $k = \lceil \log n \rceil \geq 4$*:*
$B^{(fa)}(n) = B^{(fa)}(2^{k-1} + 2^{k-4}) \leq \frac{n \lceil \log n \rceil}{2} - \frac{8n}{9}$,
$B^{(fa)}(n) = B^{(fa)}(2^{k-1} + 2^{k-3}) \leq \frac{n \lceil \log n \rceil}{2} - \frac{4n}{5}$,
$B^{(fa)}(n) = B^{(fa)}(2^{k-1} + 2^{k-2}) \leq \frac{n \lceil \log n \rceil}{2} - \frac{n}{2}$,
$B^{(fa)}(n) = B^{(fa)}(2^{k-1} + 2^{k-2} + 2^{k-3}) \leq \frac{n \lceil \log n \rceil}{2} - \frac{5n}{14}$.

Lastly, we prove the broadcast time of the hypercube under the fully-adaptive model. The Hypercube H_d of dimension d has the following set of vertices: $V_{H_d} = \{0, 1\}^d$, in which $\{0, 1\}^d$ denotes the set of binary strings with length d. Therefore, a vertex $v \in V_{H_d}$ could be represented by $\alpha = a_0a_1 \ldots a_{d-1}$, where $a_i \in \{0, 1\}, 0 \leq i \leq d-1$. The edges of H_d are denoted by E_{H_d} and it is formed as follows: A vertex $\alpha = a_0a_1 \ldots a_{d-1} \in \{0, 1\}^d$ is connected to $\alpha(i)$ for each $i \in \{0, 1, \ldots, d-1\}$, where $\alpha(i) = a_0a_1 \cdots a_{i-1}\bar{a}_i a_{i+1} \ldots a_{d-1}$. Note that $\bar{a}$ represents the binary complement of a. We call $\alpha(i)$ the ith dimensional neighbour of α. H_d has 2^d vertices, $d \cdot 2^{d-1}$ edges, diameter d, and the broadcast time of d under the classical model which is achieved as follows: The originator learns the message at time 0. Each vertex α gets informed at time $t \leq d-1$ and will call its neighbours $\alpha(t), \ldots, \alpha(d-1)$ at time $t+1, t+2, \ldots, d$, respectively.

Theorem 3 $B_{fa}(H_d) = d$

Proof The proof will directly follow from Corollary 5 by choosing G as a graph on two vertices with one edge connecting them and repeating the procedure for $d-1$ times: $(H_2, 2, 1, 1) \rightarrow (H_d, 2^d, d \cdot 2^{d-1}, d)$. The ordering of a vertex $\alpha = a_0a_1 \ldots a_{d-1}$ with fully-adaptive broadcast time of d is as follows: $\alpha :< \alpha(d-1), \ldots, \alpha(1), \alpha(0) >$, where $\alpha(i)$ is the ith dimensional neighbour of α. □

Since there exists a broadcast scheme for any hypercube on 2^d vertices that achieves $B_{fa}(H_d) = d$, and using Lemma 2, one can conclude the following:

Corollary 6 *Hypercube H_d is an mbg on 2^d vertices under $M = fa$, and $B^{(fa)}(2^k) = k \cdot 2^{k-1}$ for any $k \geq 1$.*

5 Conclusion and Future Works

We have investigated in two branches of broadcasting problem, namely universal lists and messy models. Firstly, we proposed general upper bounds on the broadcast time of a graph G under the universal lists model, and we showed that the bounds could not be improved in general. Afterward, we studied *broadcast graphs (bg)'s* and *minimum broadcast graphs (mbg)'s* under the fully-adaptive model. In particular, we presented mbg's on n vertices for $n \leq 10$ and sparse bg's for $11 \leq n \leq 14$. Using our general construction, we also suggested four infinite families of broadcast graphs under the fully-adaptive model. Lastly, we proved that Hypercube H_d is an mbg for any value of $n = 2^k$.

This study leaves several exciting research questions: The problem of finding mbg's and bg's for greater values of n under universal lists models are still widely open. Moreover, the broadcast time of several interconnection networks such as H_d are still unknown under adaptive and non-adaptive models.

A Appendix

The universal lists achieving broadcast time of $\lceil \log n \rceil$ under the fully-adaptive model for the mbg's and bg's on n vertices presented in Fig. 1:

- $\sigma_7 = \{1 :< 6, 2 >, 2 :< 3, 1 >, 3 :< 4, 2, 7 >, 4 :< 3, 5 >, 5 :< 6, 4 >, 6 :< 1, 5, 7 >, 7 :< 3, 6 >\}$,
- $\sigma_9 = \{1 :< 6, 2 >, 2 :< 3, 1 >, 3 :< 4, 2, 9 >, 4 :< 3, 5 >, 5 :< 6, 4 >, 6 :< 1, 5, 7 >, 7 :< 6, 8 >, 8 :< 7, 9 >, 9 :< 3, 8 >\}$,
- $\sigma_{10} = \{1 :< 2, 8 >, 2 :< 1, 3, 6 >, 3 :< 2, 4 >, 4 :< 5, 10, 3 >, 5 :< 4, 6 >, 6 :< 2, 5, 7 >, 7 :< 8, 6 >, 8 :< 9, 1, 7 >, 9 :< 8, 10 >, 10 :< 9, 4 >\}$.
- $\sigma_{11} = \{1 :< 7, 8, 2, 10 >, 2 :< 6, 3, 1 >, 3 :< 4, 2 >, 4 :< 3, 5, 9 >, 5 :< 11, 4, 6 >, 6 :< 5, 2, 7 >, 7 :< 6, 1 >, 8 :< 9, 11, 1 >, 9 :< 8, 4 >, 10 :< 11, 1 >, 11 :< 5, 10, 8 >\}$,
- $\sigma_{12} = \{1 :< 2, 12, 7 >, 2 :< 8, 3, 1 >, 3 :< 2, 9, 4 >, 4 :< 3, 5 >, 5 :< 11, 6, 4 >, 6 :< 12, 7, 5 >, 7 :< 6, 1, 8 >, 8 :< 2, 9, 7 >, 9 :< 8, 3, 10 >, 10 :< 11, 9 >, 11 :< 12, 5, 10 >, 12 :< 6, 1, 11 >\}$,
- $\sigma_{13} = \{1 :< 2, 6, 8 >, 2 :< 1, 3, 9 >, 3 :< 2, 4, 7, 10 >, 4 :< 3, 5, 11 >, 5 :< 4, 6, 12 >, 6 :< 5, 1, 7, 13 >, 7 :< 9, 6, 11, 3, 13 >, 8 :< 13, 9, 1 >, 9 :< 8, 10, 2, 7 >, 10 :< 9, 11, 3 >, 11 :< 10, 12, 4, 7 >, 12 :< 11, 13, 5 >, 13 :< 12, 8, 6, 7 >\}$,
- $\sigma_{14} = \{1 :< 6, 2, 8 >, 2 :< 3, 1, 9 >, 3 :< 4, 2, 7, 10 >, 4 :< 3, 5, 11 >, 5 :< 6, 4, 12 >, 6 :< 1, 5, 7, 13 >, 7 :< 3, 6, 14 >, 8 :< 13, 9, 1 >, 9 :< 10, 8, 2 >, 10 :< 11, 9, 14, 3 >, 11 :< 10, 12, 4 >, 12 :< 13, 11, 5 >, 13 :< 8, 12, 14, 6 >, 14 :< 10, 13, 7 >\}$.

References

1. Ahlswede, R., Haroutunian, H., Khachatrian, L.H.: Messy broadcasting in networks. In: Communications and Cryptography, pp. 13–24. Springer (1994)
2. Al Faisal, F., Rahman, M.H., Inoguchi, Y.: A new power efficient high performance interconnection network for many-core processors. Journal of Parallel and Distributed Computing **101**, 92–102 (2017)
3. Barsky, G., Grigoryan, H., Harutyunyan, H.A.: Tight lower bounds on broadcast function for n= 24 and 25. Discrete Applied Mathematics **175**, 109–114 (2014)
4. Bermond, J.C., Hell, P., Liestman, A.L., Peters, J.G.: Sparse broadcast graphs. Discrete applied mathematics **36**(2), 97–130 (1992)
5. Comellas, F., Harutyunyan, H.A., Liestman, A.L.: Messy broadcasting in multidimensional directed tori. Journal of Interconnection Networks **4**(01), 37–51 (2003)
6. Diks, K., Pelc, A.: Broadcasting with universal lists. Networks **27**(3), 183–196 (1996)
7. Dinneen, M.J.: The complexity of broadcasting in bounded-degree networks. arXiv preprint math/9411222 (1994)
8. Dinneen, M.J., Fellows, M.R., Faber, V.: Algebraic constructions of efficient broadcast networks. In: International Symposium on Applied Algebra, Algebraic Algorithms, and Error-Correcting Codes. pp. 152–158. Springer (1991)

9. Elkin, M., Kortsarz, G.: Sublogarithmic approximation for telephone multicast: path out of jungle. In: SODA. vol. 3, pp. 76–85 (2003)
10. Farley, A.M., Hedetniemi, S.T., Mitchell, S., Proskurowski, A.: Minimum broadcast graphs. Discret. Math. **25**(2), 189–193 (1979)
11. Fraigniaud, P., Lazard, E.: Methods and problems of communication in usual networks. Discrete Applied Mathematics **53**(1), 79–133 (1994). https://doi.org/10.1016/0166-218X(94)90180-5. https://www.sciencedirect.com/science/article/pii/0166218X94901805
12. Fraigniaud, P., Vial, S.: Approximation algorithms for broadcasting and gossiping. Journal of Parallel and Distributed Computing **43**(1), 47–55 (1997)
13. Gholami, S., Harutyunyan, H.A.: A broadcasting heuristic for hypercube of trees. In: 2021 IEEE 11th Annual Computing and Communication Workshop and Conference (CCWC). pp. 0355–0361. IEEE (2021)
14. Gholami, S, Harutyunyan, H.A, Maraachlian, E.: Optimal broadcasting in fully connected trees. J. Interconnection Netw., 2150037 (2022)
15. Gholami, S., Harutyunyan, H.A.: Fully-adaptive model for broadcasting with universal lists. In: 244th International Symposium on Symbolic and Numeric Algorithms for Scientific Computing (SYNASC). IEEE (2022)
16. Harutyunyan, H.A., Liestman, A.L.: Messy broadcasting. Parallel Processing Letters **8**(02), 149–159 (1998)
17. Harutyunyan, H.A., Liestman, A.L., Makino, K., Shermer, T.C.: Nonadaptive broadcasting in trees. Networks **57**(2), 157–168 (2011)
18. Harutyunyan, H.A., Liestman, A.L., Peters, J.G., Richards, D.: Broadcasting and gossiping. Handbook of Graph Theorey pp. 1477–1494 (2013)
19. Harutyunyan, H.A., Maraachlian, E.: On broadcasting in unicyclic graphs. Journal of combinatorial optimization **16**(3), 307–322 (2008)
20. Harutyunyan, H.A., Shao, B.: An efficient heuristic for broadcasting in networks. Journal of Parallel and Distributed Computing **66**(1), 68–76 (2006)
21. Hedetniemi, S.M., Hedetniemi, S.T., Liestman, A.L.: A survey of gossiping and broadcasting in communication networks. Networks **18**(4), 319–349 (1988)
22. Hromkovič, J., Klasing, R., Monien, B., Peine, R.: Dissemination of information in interconnection networks (broadcasting & gossiping). In: Combinatorial network theory, pp. 125–212. Springer (1996)
23. Jakoby, A., Reischuk, R., Schindelhauer, C.: The complexity of broadcasting in planar and decomposable graphs. Discrete Applied Mathematics **83**(1–3), 179–206 (1998)
24. Khachatrian, L., Harutounian, O.: Construction of new classes of minimal broadcast networks. In: Conference on Coding Theory, Armenia. pp. 69–77 (1990)
25. Kim, J.H., Chwa, K.Y.: Optimal broadcasting with universal lists based on competitive analysis. Networks **45**(4), 224–231 (2005)
26. Knodel, W.: New gossips and telephones. Discrete Mathematics **13**, 95 (1975)
27. Kortsarz, G., Peleg, D.: Approximation algorithms for minimum-time broadcast. SIAM Journal on Discrete Mathematics **8**(3), 401–427 (1995)
28. Lewis, H.R.: Computers and intractability. a guide to the theory of np-completeness (1983)
29. Li, C., Hart, T.E., Henry, K.J., Neufeld, I.A.: Average-case" messy" broadcasting. Journal of Interconnection Networks **9**(04), 487–505 (2008)
30. Maheo, M., Saclé, J.F.: Some minimum broadcast graphs. Discrete Applied Mathematics **53**(1–3), 275–285 (1994)
31. Ravi, R.: Rapid rumor ramification: Approximating the minimum broadcast time. In: Proceedings 35th Annual Symposium on Foundations of Computer Science (FOCS). pp. 202–213. IEEE (1994)
32. Rocher-Gonzalez, J., Escudero-Sahuquillo, J., García, P.J., Quiles, F.J.: On the impact of routing algorithms in the effectiveness of queuing schemes in high-performance interconnection networks. In: 2017 IEEE 25th Annual Symposium on High-Performance Interconnects (HOTI). pp. 65–72. IEEE (2017)

33. Rosenthal, A., Scheuermann, P.: Universal rankings for broadcasting in tree networks. In: Proceedings of the 25th Allerton Conference on Communication, Control and Computing. pp. 641–649 (1987)
34. Saclé, J.F.: Lower bounds for the size in four families of minimum broadcast graphs. Discrete Mathematics **150**(1–3), 359–369 (1996)
35. Slater, P.J., Cockayne, E.J., Hedetniemi, S.T.: Information dissemination in trees. SIAM Journal on Computing **10**(4), 692–701 (1981)

Investigating the Origins of Fractality Based on Two Novel Fractal Network Models

Enikő Zakar-Polyák, Marcell Nagy, and Roland Molontay

Abstract Numerous network models have been investigated to gain insights into the origins of fractality. In this work, we introduce two novel network models, to better understand the growing mechanism and structural characteristics of fractal networks. The Repulsion Based Fractal Model (RBFM) is built on the well-known Song-Havlin-Makse (SHM) model, but in RBFM repulsion is always present among a specific group of nodes. The model resolves the contradiction between the SHM model and the Hub Attraction Dynamical Growth model, by showing that repulsion is the characteristic that induces fractality. The Lattice Small-world Transition Model (LSwTM) was motivated by the fact that repulsion directly influences the node distances. Through LSwTM we study the fractal-small-world transition. The model illustrates the transition on a fixed number of nodes and edges using a preferential-attachment-based edge rewiring process. It shows that a small average distance works against fractal scaling, and also demonstrates that fractality is not a dichotomous property, continuous transition can be observed between the pure fractal and non-fractal characteristics.

1 Introduction

Modelling real networks has attracted a great deal of research in the last two decades since mathematical models allow us to rigorously and extensively investigate the underlying mechanisms of networks, discover substantial network properties, and shed light on their origins. For example, the preferential attachment model of Barabási and Albert explained the origin of the scale-free property [1], the model of Watts and Strogatz helped in understanding the "small-world" phenomena in a variety of

E. Zakar-Polyák · M. Nagy · R. Molontay (✉)
Department of Stochastics, Institute of Mathematics, Budapest University of Technology and Economics, Műegyetem rkp. 3., H-1111, Budapest, Hungary
e-mail: molontay@math.bme.hu

R. Molontay
ELKH-BME Stochastics Research Group, Műegyetem rkp. 3., H-1111, Budapest, Hungary

D. Pacheco et al. (eds.), *Complex Networks XIII*, Springer Proceedings in Complexity,
https://doi.org/10.1007/978-3-031-17658-6_4

networks [17], while the model of Newman provided a better understanding of the properties of highly clustered networks [9].

Fractality is another well-studied property, which is present in a large number of real networks [10, 18]. Fractal scaling of networks has been introduced by Song et al. [13] motivated by the notion of geometric fractals. Fractality is defined by the so-called box-covering method. A network is called fractal, if the minimum number of boxes required to cover the whole vertex set follows a power-law relation with the size of the boxes, i.e.:

$$N_B(l_B) \sim l_B^{-d_B},$$

where l_B denotes the size of the boxes, $N_B(l_B)$ stands for the number of l_B-sized boxes resulting from box-covering, and d_B is called the box-dimension or fractal dimension of the network (if exists).

After laying the foundation of fractal network analysis, Song et al. also proposed a mathematical model to explain the emergence of fractality in complex networks [14]. The main steps of the Song-Havlin-Makse (SHM) model can be summarised as follows:

1. The initial graph is a simple structure, e.g., two nodes connected via a link.
2. In iteration step $t + 1$ we connect m offspring to both endpoints of every edge, i.e., a v node gains $m \cdot \deg_t(v)$ offspring, where m is a predefined parameter and $\deg_t(v)$ is the degree of node v at the end of step t.
3. In iteration step $t + 1$ every (u, v) edge is removed independently with probability p, where p is a predefined parameter. When an edge is removed, it is replaced with a new edge between random offspring of u and v.

The network grows dynamically and the degree correlation (hub repulsion/attraction) of the emerging graph is driven by parameter p. The fractality is also influenced by the choice of parameter p, namely, it can be shown that the generated network is fractal for $p = 1$, and non-fractal for $p = 0$ [14]. The intermediate values develop mixtures between the two properties. The authors conclude that the "repulsion-between-hubs" principle is the key to the emergence of fractal scaling [14].

Kuang et al. proposed the Hub Attraction Dynamical Growth (HADG) model, which is a modification of the SHM model, where the novelty lies in the flexible edge rewiring probability [7]. They demonstrated that by assigning smaller rewiring probability to edges connecting hubs, it is possible to create fractal networks with hub attraction behaviour. They also introduced a so-called "within-box link-growth" phase to the model to increase the clustering coefficient of the resulting network, which does not affect the fractal scaling [7].

Besides the relation of hub repulsion/disassortativity to fractality, another interesting phenomenon to model has been the conflicting relation of fractality and the small-world property [6]. For example, Rozenfeld et al. proposed a new family of recursive networks, which are small-world for certain parameter settings, and fractal for others [11]. There are also many articles, which introduce models that exhibit a transition between the two properties [8, 12, 16, 20].

In this work, we introduce two novel fractal network models. First, we present the Repulsion Based Fractal Model (RBFM), which is intended to resolve the seeming contradiction of [7, 14] by showing that repulsion causes the fractality of both the SHM and HADG models. Motivated by the fact that repulsion between nodes inevitably increases the average shortest path distance of a network, we introduce a second model to study the relationship between fractality and small-worldness. The second model, called Lattice Small-world Transition Model (LSwTM), supports the findings of earlier works [8, 12, 16] that small-world property interferes with fractality, and that real transition exists between the two characteristics. In contrast to the related works, our model is not relying on the normalisation method, and LSwTM is not a growing network, but the transition is shown on a fixed number of edges and nodes.

2 Repulsion Based Fractal Model

This model is based on the Song-Havlin-Makse model, it also evolves through time, and we rewire edges to create repulsion among nodes. However, here the probability of an edge to be rewired is not fixed but depends on the degree of its endpoints. In contrast to the Song-Havlin-Makse model, repulsion is always present in RBFM, moreover, with a predefined parameter we can specify the nodes that repel each other (e.g., hubs or small degree nodes). The model also adapts the "within-box link-growth" step of Kuang et al. [7] in order to create more realistic networks. The growing mechanism of the Repulsion Based Fractal Model is as follows:

1. Similarly to the Song-Havlin-Makse model, we start with a simple graph structure, e.g. two nodes connected via a link.
2. The growth process of the model is the same as step 2 of the SHM model, namely in iteration step $t+1$ we connect $m \cdot \deg_t(v)$ offspring to every v node, where m is a predefined parameter and $\deg_t(v)$ is the degree of node v at the end of step t.
3. In iteration step $t+1$ we remove every (u, v) edge with probability p_{uv}^Y that depends on the mean degree of u and v normalised by the maximum degree:

$$p_{uv}^Y = 1 - \left| Y - \frac{\deg_t(u) + \deg_t(v)}{2 \cdot \deg_{t,\max}} \right|,$$

   where $Y \in [0, 1]$ is a predefined parameter, $\deg_t(u)$ is the degree of node u, $\deg_{t,\max}$ is the maximum degree at step t. When an edge is removed, it is replaced with a uniformly randomly chosen new edge between the offspring of its endpoints.
4. We add $\deg_t(v)$ edges among the newly generated offspring of every old node v. In order not to create self-loops this step is only executed, when $m > 1$.

With the Y parameter, we assign high edge rewiring probability to those edges, which endpoints' average degree is close to $Y \cdot \deg_{t,\max}$. For example, if $Y = 0$, with

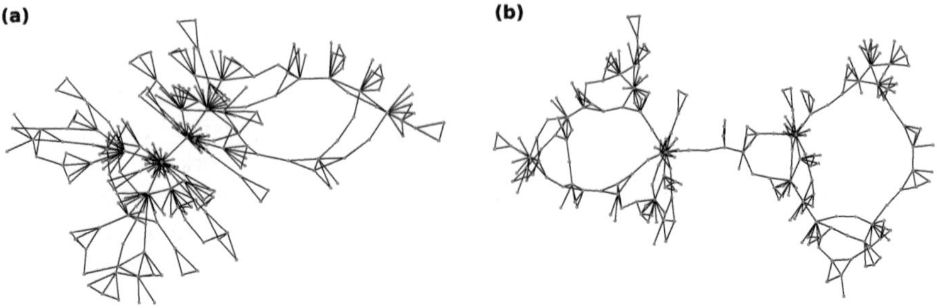

Fig. 1 Illustration of the Repulsion Based Fractal Model for (**a**) $Y = 0$, i.e., when small degree nodes tend to repel each other, (**b**) $Y = 1$, i.e., when the repulsion is present among hubs

high probability we rewire those edges, which connect nodes with a relatively small degree, on the other hand in the case of $Y = 1$, with high probability we rewire the edges, that are linked between nodes with large degree (hubs). Figure 1 illustrates these two extreme cases of the model. The speciality of this model, is that it gives rise to fractal graphs for all $Y \in [0, 1]$, as it can be seen on Fig. 2(a), too.

According to Song et al. [14] fractality is driven by disassortativity (negative degree correlation), however, Kuang et al. [7] introduced a model that generates fractal networks where the hubs are connected. The Repulsion Based Fractal (RBF) Model suggests that the property, which affects the fractal scaling of a network is "repulsion", and repulsion does not necessarily have to be among hubs. The resolution of the contradiction lies in the fact that repulsion clearly affects the correlation of degrees. If there is a repulsion between hubs, i.e., if in the RBF model $Y = 1$, then hubs are only connected with small degree nodes, thus the degrees are anti-correlated and the network is disassortative. On the other hand, when the repulsion is between the small degree nodes, there are long paths consisting of small degree nodes, but in this case, the hubs are connected, hence there is a significantly larger correlation between the degrees. However, the resulting network is still fractal. The common mechanism that drives the fractality of the Song-Havlin-Makse model [14], the model of Kuang et al. [7], and the RBFM is repulsion.

Clearly, repulsion makes the graphs spread out, i.e., when the nodes are repelling each other, then the graph cannot be too compact. To study the relationship between small-worldness and fractality we introduce the Lattice Small-world Transition model that is detailed in Sect. 3.

2.1 Properties of the RBFM

Some of the main properties of the networks generated by the Repulsion Based Fractal Model are deterministic, i.e., do not depend on the exact realisations, but are determined by the parameters. In fact, the number of nodes and edges of the network are only influenced by the choice of parameter m and the number of iterations t. Following the notations and thread of [7, 14] we can conclude the following for the $m > 1$ case of the model:

$$\begin{aligned} E(t) - E(t-1) &= 2m \cdot E(t-1) + 2 \cdot E(t-1) \\ E(t) &= (2m+3) \cdot E(t-1) = E(0) \cdot (2m+3)^t, \end{aligned}$$

where $E(t)$ denotes the number of edges of the network at step t, while $E(0)$ is the number of edges of the initial graph. For the number of nodes the following findings can be made:

$$\begin{aligned} N(t) - N(t-1) &= 2m \cdot E(t-1) \\ N(t) &= N(t-1) + 2m \cdot E(0) \cdot (2m+3)^{t-1} \\ &= N(0) + E(0) \cdot 2m \cdot \sum_{k=0}^{t-1} (2m+3)^k \\ &= N(0) + E(0) \cdot \frac{m}{m+1} \cdot ((2m+3)^t - 1), \end{aligned}$$

where $N(t)$ refers to the number of nodes of the network at iteration step t, and $N(0)$ is the number of nodes of the initial graph.

When $m = 1$, step 4 cannot be executed, consequently the previous derivations simplify:

$$\begin{aligned} E(t) - E(t-1) &= 2m \cdot E(t-1) \\ E(t) &= E(0) \cdot (2m+1)^t = E(0) \cdot 3^t \\ N(t) &= N(0) + E(0) \cdot 2m \cdot \sum_{k=0}^{t-1} (2m+1)^k \\ &= N(0) + E(0) \cdot ((2m+1)^t - 1) = N(0) + E(0) \cdot (3^t - 1) \end{aligned}$$

Since the number of nodes and edges are deterministic in parameters m and t, the average degree of the network can also be studied analytically. In the $m = 1$ case:

$$d_{avg} = \frac{2 \cdot E(0) \cdot 3^t}{N(0) + E(0) \cdot (3^t - 1)} \xrightarrow[t \to \infty]{} 2$$

When $m > 1$:

$$d_{avg} = \frac{2 \cdot E(0) \cdot (2m+3)^t}{N(0) + E(0) \cdot \frac{m}{m+1} \cdot ((2m+3)^t - 1)} \xrightarrow[t \to \infty]{} \frac{2(m+1)}{m} \xrightarrow[m \to \infty]{} 2$$

To investigate how similar the random realisations instead of generalisations of the model with a given parameter setting are in terms of various network characteristics, we generated 30 graphs with a given parameter setting. We examined 7 network metrics, namely, the average path length, the normalised diameter, the normalised maximum degree, the average clustering coefficient, the assortativity coefficient, the maximum of the eigenvector centralities, and the skewness of the degree distribution. The results can be found in the supplementary material: https://github.com/marcessz/fractal-network-models. The examined characteristics can be considered stable because the values of the metrics do not differ significantly for the different realisations of the networks. The average clustering coefficient, and also the maximum of the eigenvector centralities may not seem to be as consistent as the other metrics, but the range, in which the values vary is still quite small. Furthermore, the fluctuation decreases for larger networks, i.e., when the model performs more iterations. Overall, we can conclude that the main characteristics of the network model for a given parameter setting do not depend heavily on the exact realisations.

We also investigated how sensitive the model is to its parameters, i.e., how a small change in the parameters affects the characteristics of the network. Due to the complicated network evolution process, it is difficult to analytically determine various characteristics of the model, thus we generated 30 graphs with a certain parameter setting and averaged the graph metrics of these 30 realisations. We repeated this procedure for various parameter settings to assess the parameter sensitivity of the model. Figure 2(b), (c), (d) show the contour plots of three network metrics (assortativity, maximum eigenvector centrality, average clustering coefficient). It can be seen that some of the characteristics do not, or just barely depend on the choice of parameter Y, while others are highly influenced by it. The average clustering coefficient is quite non-sensitive for all of the parameters, but naturally increases greatly, when the structure of the network is more complex than a path (i.e., when $m > 1$). The other examined characteristics highly depend on the realisation of parameter Y. The average path length and the (normalised) diameter become larger as we increase the value of Y, and similar holds for the maximal eigenvector centrality. The generated networks are disassortative in all of the cases, but the model gets more disassortative for larger values of Y, i.e. when the repulsion is created among large degree nodes.

3 Lattice Small-World Transition Model

Our novel model embraces both preferential attachment mechanism and the "geometric" structure that emerges in networks that can be embedded in two- and three-dimensional Euclidean spaces, for instance, infrastructure networks [2], blood vessels, and trabecular bones [19]. Several network models have been introduced to create a synergy between geometric network models and preferential attachment. For example, Flaxman et al. have presented two growth models in which the vertices of the network are randomly chosen points of the three-dimensional unit sphere, and edges are created taking into account both the proximity of the nodes and an extended preferential

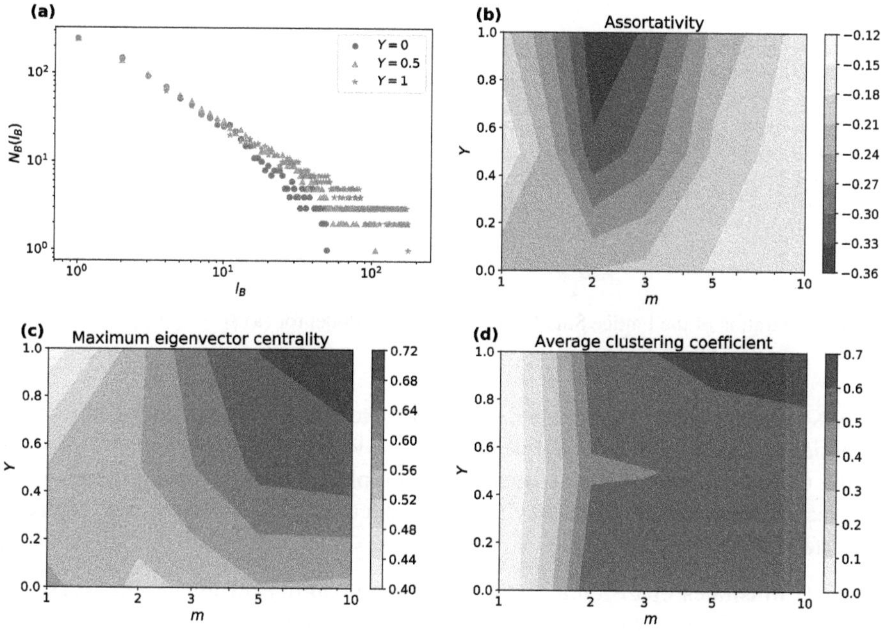

Fig. 2 (**a**) Illustration of the fractality of the Repulsion Based Fractal Model for different parameter settings. (**b**)–(**d**) Contour plots of three network metrics, which show the change of the metric values as a function of parameters m and Y of the Repulsion Based Fractal Model. The subfigures illustrate the values of the (**b**) assortativity coefficient, (**c**) maximal eigenvector centrality, (**d**) average clustering coefficient for networks generated by the model with $t = 3$ setting and with multiple choices of parameters m and Y

attachment mechanism [3, 4]. The use of the preferential attachment principle to create small-world networks has also been studied extensively [5, 15].

Here, we present a network model, which utilises the fractal nature of grid-like structures, and at the same time works against it with the preferential attachment mechanism. The Lattice Small-world Transition Model is defined as follows:

1. We start with a d-dimensional (practically $d = 2$) grid graph with $n_1 \times n_2 \times \cdots \times n_d$ vertices.
2. With probability p, every (v_i, v_j) edge is replaced by (v_i, v_k), where v_k is chosen with a probability, that is proportional to p_{v_k}:

$$p_{v_k} = \frac{1}{1 + \exp\left(-a \cdot \left(\frac{\deg(v_k)}{\deg_{\max}} - \frac{1}{2}\right)\right)},$$

where a is a positive constant, $\deg(v_k)$ is the degree of node v_k and $\deg_{\max}$ is the maximum degree of the current graph. Note that when the normalised degree of v_k is $\frac{1}{2}$, then p_{v_k} equals $\frac{1}{2}$. If $\deg(v_k)$ is less than $\deg_{\max}/2$, then p_{v_k} is close to zero, on the other hand, when $\deg(v_k) > \deg_{\max}/2$ then p_{v_k} is nearly one (if

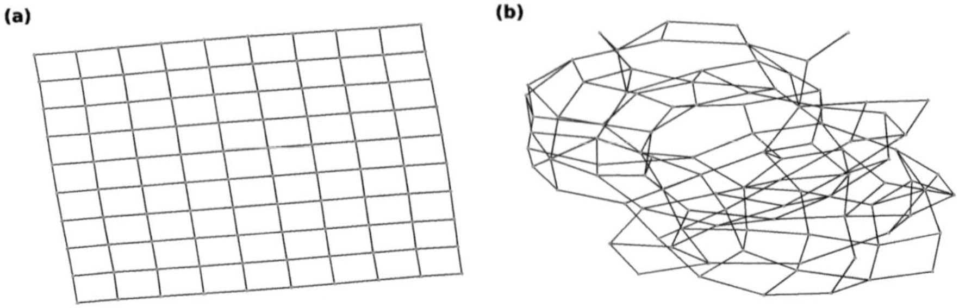

Fig. 3 Illustration of the Lattice Small-world Transition Model for (**a**) $p = 0$, (**b**) $p = 0.1$

a is large enough). By practical motivation, to avoid multiple edges, the set of nodes to select v_k from is defined as $S_{v_i} = V \setminus \{\Gamma_{v_i} \cup \{v_i\}\}$, where Γ_{v_i} denotes the neighbourhood of v_i. By default, v_j is replaced with v_k during the rewiring process, however, if in this way the graph becomes disconnected, v_i is replaced instead.

Figure 3 illustrates that even a small rewiring probability results in a network that differs greatly from a grid graph. The fractality of the generated network depends on the choice of p. For $p = 0$ the network is purely fractal, and as p grows the model shows a transition from fractal to non-fractal. It also has to be mentioned that this transition is not sharp, and there are intermediate states, where the network is locally fractal, although the pure property is no longer present globally. These properties are well illustrated on Fig. 5(a). Furthermore, as fractality disappears small-world property arises. Figure 4 shows the change in the normalised diameter and average path length in terms of the model parameters. The normalisation by the logarithm of the number of nodes is done to be able to compare the distances of networks of different sizes. It can be seen that the distances are growing as p decreases, i.e., as the networks become fractal. Both RBFM and LSwTM suggest that a fractal network has to be spread out, and as LSwTM illustrates, as we rewire edges according to the preferential attachment mechanism, it turns small-world and loses its fractal structure.

3.1 Properties of the LSwTM

Similarly to the RBFM, some properties of the networks generated by the Lattice Small-world Transition Model are deterministic in the model parameters. The number of nodes and edges of a grid graph is determined by its n_i $(i = 1, 2, \ldots, d)$ parameters. Since the model only includes edge rewiring steps and there is no edge/node deletion or addition, the resulting network has the same number of nodes and edges as the initial graph.

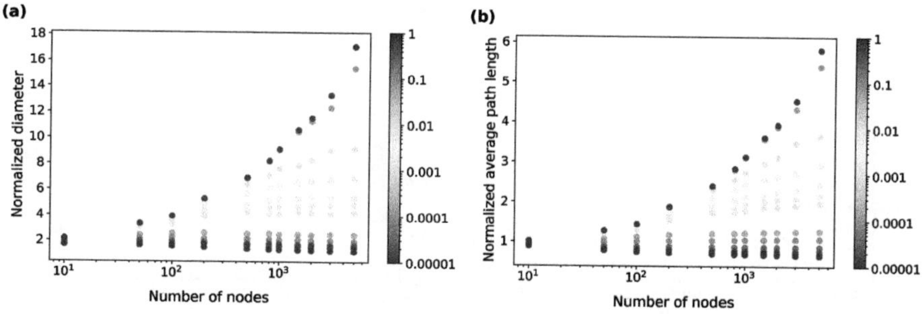

Fig. 4 (**a**) Normalised diameter and (**b**) average path length (i.e. diameter/average path length divided by the logarithm of the size) as a function of the logarithm of the number of nodes. The colouring is based on the p parameter of the model

Simple derivations can be made for the number of nodes and edges of the generated networks, when the initial grid graph is d-dimensional, i.e when we have parameters $n_1, n_2, \ldots, n_d$:

$$|V| = \prod_{i=1}^{d} n_i$$

$$|E| = \sum_{i=1}^{d} (n_i - 1) \cdot \frac{\prod_{j=1}^{d} n_j}{n_i}$$

$$d_{avg} = \frac{2 \cdot \sum_{i=1}^{d} (n_i - 1) \cdot \frac{\prod_{j=1}^{d} n_j}{n_i}}{\prod_{i=1}^{d} n_i} = \frac{2 \cdot \left(\sum_{i=1}^{d} \prod_{j=1}^{d} n_j - \sum_{i=1}^{d} \frac{\prod_{j=1}^{d} n_j}{n_i} \right)}{\prod_{i=1}^{d} n_i}$$
$$= 2d - 2 \cdot \sum_{i=1}^{d} \frac{1}{n_i}$$

When all n_is are large, the average degree is close to $2d$. On the other hand, when $n_i = 2$ for all $i = 1, 2, \ldots, d$, the average degree equals to d. Consequently, if $n_i > 1$ for all i, the following bounds hold: $d \leq d_{avg} < 2d$. If $n_i = 1$ for at least one i, the average degree can be smaller than d, since in this case we basically start with a lattice of dimension less than d.

We also investigated how similar the random realisations of the LSwTM are, moreover we also executed a sensitivity analysis on the parameters of the model. Again, we consider the same seven structural network metrics as before. For a given parameter setting the generated networks have very similar properties concerning the examined characteristics. The results can be found in the supplementary material: https://github.com/marcessz/fractal-network-models.

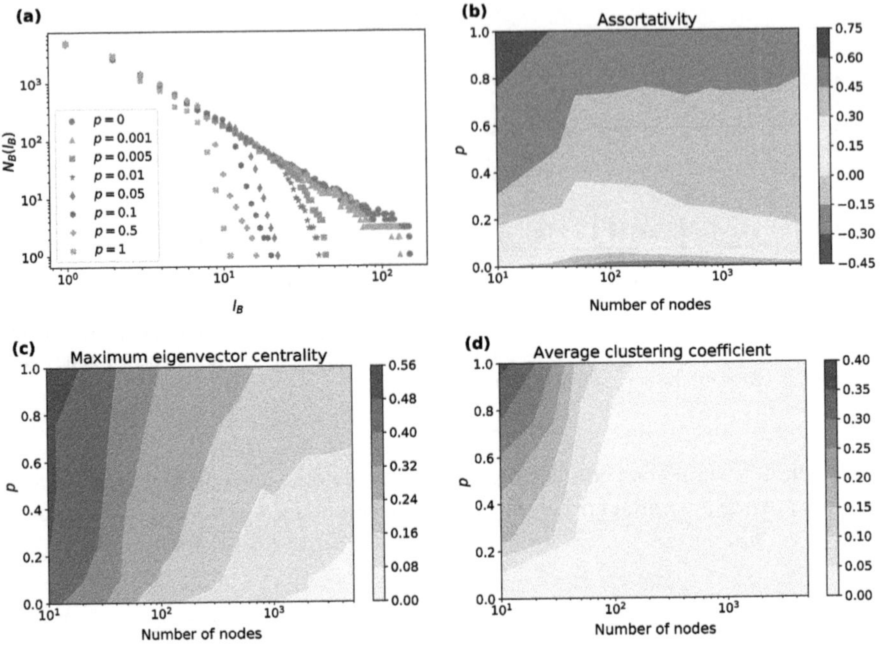

Fig. 5 (**a**) Illustration of the fractality of the LSwT model for different parameter settings. (**b**)–(**d**) Contour plots of three graph metrics, illustrating the metric values as a function of the parameters of the LSwTM. The subfigures illustrate the values of the (**b**) assortativity coefficient, (**c**) maximal eigenvector centrality, (**d**) average clustering coefficient for networks generated by the model with multiple choices of the number of the nodes and parameter p

Figure 5(b), (c), (d) show how the model parameters affect some characteristics of the network. Most of the graph metrics are influenced mainly by the network size, for example, the maximal eigenvector centrality decreases as the network grows. The average clustering coefficient, apart from the small networks, is around 0, independently of the value of p. Some characteristics, however, rather depend on parameter p and are not affected highly by the network size. The assortativity coefficient decreases with the growing values of p, and the same holds for the average path length and the (normalised) diameter too, with the remark that these two become small even for values of p slightly greater than 0.

4 Discussion and Summary

In this work, we introduced and analysed two network models to better understand what mechanisms affect the fractality of networks.

The Repulsion Based Fractal Model is based on the models of Song et al. [14] and Kuang et al. [7]. Song et al. assumed that in fractal networks the hubs are not connected, in other words, there is a repulsion between hubs, which is also known as disassortative mixing. On the other hand, Kuang et al. modified the Song-Havlin-Makse model, in such a way that it is able to generate fractal networks with connected hubs. Although Kuang et al. pointed out that disassortativity is not the mechanism that makes a network fractal, they did not investigate thoroughly the origins of fractality. Through the Repulsion Based Fractal Model, we showed that the repulsion between nodes induces fractality, and the repelling nodes do not necessarily have to be hubs. The RBF model also well illustrates that repulsion affects not only the fractality but the assortative-mixing of a network, which resolves the contradiction between the findings of Song et al. [14] and Kuang et al. [7].

As the RBFM and earlier works suggest [8, 12, 16, 20], fractality is influenced by the node distances. We introduced a model, which shows that if we take a purely fractal network, and we start to rewire edges according to the preferential attachment principle, then as the shortest path length decreases, the fractal structure breaks down gradually, and eventually the small-world property will dominate the network.

References

1. Barabási, A.L., Albert, R.: Emergence of scaling in random networks. Science **286**(5439), 509–512 (1999). https://doi.org/10.1126/science.286.5439.509
2. Csányi, G., Szendrői, B.: Fractal-small-world dichotomy in real-world networks. Phys. Rev. E **70**(1), 016122 (2004). https://doi.org/10.1103/PhysRevE.70.016122
3. Flaxman, A.D., Frieze, A.M., Vera, J.: A geometric preferential attachment model of networks. Internet Math. **3**(2), 187–205 (2006). https://doi.org/10.1080/15427951.2006.10129124
4. Flaxman, A.D., Frieze, A.M., Vera, J.: A geometric preferential attachment model of networks II. Internet Math. **4**(1), 87–111 (2007). https://doi.org/10.1080/15427951.2007.10129137
5. Jian-Guo, L., Yan-Zhong, D., Zhong-Tuo, W.: Multistage random growing small-world networks with power-law degree distribution. Chin. Phys. Lett. **23**(3), 746 (2006). https://doi.org/10.1088/0256-307X/23/3/061
6. Kawasaki, F., Yakubo, K.: Reciprocal relation between the fractal and the small-world properties of complex networks. Phys. Rev. E **82**(3), 036113 (2010). https://doi.org/10.1103/PhysRevE.82.036113
7. Kuang, L., Zheng, B., Li, D., Li, Y., Sun, Y.: A fractal and scale-free model of complex networks with hub attraction behaviors. Sci. China Inf. Sci. **58**(1), 1–10 (2015). https://doi.org/10.1007/s11432-014-5115-7
8. Li, D., Wang, X., Huang, P.: A fractal growth model: exploring the connection pattern of hubs in complex networks. Phys. Stat. Mech. Appl. **471**, 200–211 (2017). https://doi.org/10.1016/j.physa.2016.12.038
9. Newman, M.E.: Properties of highly clustered networks. Phys. Rev. E **68**(2), 026121 (2003). https://doi.org/10.1103/PhysRevE.68.026121
10. Rosenberg, E.: Fractal Dimensions of Networks. Springer, Berlin (2020). https://doi.org/10.1007/978-3-030-43169-3
11. Rozenfeld, H.D., Havlin, S., Ben-Avraham, D.: Fractal and transfractal recursive scale-free nets. New J. Phys. **9**(6), 175 (2007). https://doi.org/10.1088/1367-2630/9/6/175
12. Rozenfeld, H.D., Song, C., Makse, H.A.: Small-world to fractal transition in complex networks: a renormalization group approach. Phys. Rev. Lett. **104**(2), 025701 (2010). https://doi.org/10.1103/PhysRevLett.104.025701

13. Song, C., Havlin, S., Makse, H.A.: Self-similarity of complex networks. Nature **433**(7024), 392–395 (2005). https://doi.org/10.1038/nature03248
14. Song, C., Havlin, S., Makse, H.A.: Origins of fractality in the growth of complex networks. Nat. Phys. **2**(4), 275–281 (2006). https://doi.org/10.1038/nphys266
15. Wang, J., Rong, L.: Evolving small-world networks based on the modified BA model. In: 2008 International Conference on Computer Science and Information Technology, pp. 143–146. IEEE (2008). https://doi.org/10.1109/ICCSIT.2008.119
16. Watanabe, A., Mizutaka, S., Yakubo, K.: Fractal and small-world networks formed by self-organized critical dynamics. J. Phys. Soc. Jpn. **84**(11), 114003 (2015). https://doi.org/10.7566/JPSJ.84.114003
17. Watts, D.J., Strogatz, S.H.: Collective dynamics o "small-world" networks. Nature **393**(6684), 440–442 (1998). https://doi.org/10.1038/30918
18. Wen, T., Cheong, K.H.: The fractal dimension of complex networks: a review. Inf. Fusion **73**, 87–102 (2021). https://doi.org/10.1016/j.inffus.2021.02.001
19. Wlczek, P., Odgaard, A., Sernetz, M.: Fractal 3d analysis of blood vessels and bones. In: Fractal Geometry and Computer Graphics, pp. 240–248. Springer, Berlin (1992). https://doi.org/10.1007/978-3-642-95678-2_19
20. Zhang, Z., Zhou, S., Chen, L., Guan, J.: Transition from fractal to non-fractal scalings in growing scale-free networks. Eur. Phys. J. B **64**(2), 277–283 (2008). https://doi.org/10.1140/epjb/e2008-00299-1

A Data-Driven Approach to Cattle Epidemic Modelling Under Uncertainty

Sima Farokhnejad, Denis Cardoso, Christiane Rocha, Angélica S. da Mata, and Ronaldo Menezes

Abstract Cattle movement is an intrinsic part of animal husbandry (i.e., breeding, maintenance, slaughter of livestock). There are an estimated 1 billion cattle heads in the world used for the production of meat, milk, leather, among other products, which are consumed by billions of people. The pressures of efficiently delivering animal products to individuals, lead to a stress in the system both in the number of heads kept and traded, and in the number of possible contacts between these heads. Under these conditions, contact tracing and avoidance is an essential part of modern agriculture because highly contagious diseases such as brucellosis and foot-and-mouth disease can spread through contact, leading to heavy economic costs. Many countries track their cattle with electronic tags (e.g. Australia, Canada) which leads to a highly-precise monitoring capability. Unfortunately, several of the largest producers in the world (e.g. Brazil, Mexico, USA), do not mandate such use, and some do not even mandate the tracking of animal movement (e.g. Mexico, USA). Added to this, the lack of tracking capabilities enable people to take advantage of the system by engaging in unregulated cattle trade. The consequence is that official movement data may contain uncertainty in the number of cattle movements as well as the number of actual trades. This work focuses on understanding uncertainty in cattle movement networks and its relation to epidemic modelling.

1 Introduction

Cattle products such as dairy, beef, and leather are consumed around the world, making it a very valuable commodity. In 2018, 71 million tones of beef products were produced[1] with the USA, Brazil, China, India, Argentina and Australia as

[1] https://ourworldindata.org/meat-production (last accessed: 23 May 2022).

S. Farokhnejad · A. S. da Mata · R. Menezes (✉)
Department of Computer Science, University of Exeter, Exeter, England, UK
e-mail: r.menezes@exeter.ac.uk

D. Cardoso · C. Rocha
Department of Veterinary Medicine, Federal University of Lavras, Lavras, MG, Brazil

D. Pacheco et al. (eds.), *Complex Networks XIII*, Springer Proceedings in Complexity,
https://doi.org/10.1007/978-3-031-17658-6_5

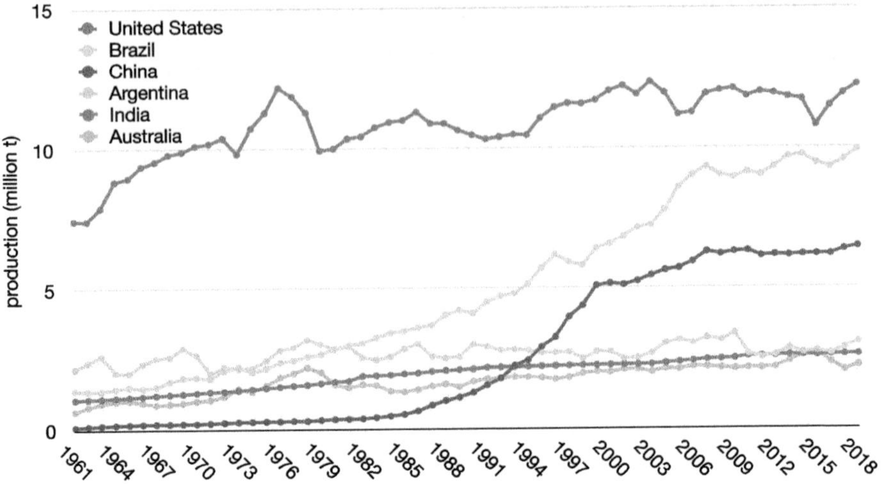

Fig. 1 The production of meat by livestock type (beef and buffalo) for the 6-large producers in the world. The chart clearly shows a different growth rate for Brazil and China when compared to other countries

the top-6 producers, in this order. From these, Fig. 1 shows that the growth rate in the production in Brazil and China differs significantly from other places (e.g. the production in Europe has almost halved since 1990s).

The rate of production in Brazil and China should be accompanied by mechanisms to avoid epidemics of conditions such as brucellosis and foot-and-mouth disease (FMD), as an outbreak can have serious financial consequences for the producers and to the countries. The 2001 FMD epidemic in the UK is probably one of the best-documented livestock epidemics. It has been reported that about 3 million animals were slaughtered as a result of the epidemic; 6% of the national livestock herd. The farms were affected directly and sustained severe losses of £84 million, in addition to the actual killing of all their livestock [8].

Besides avoiding an economic crisis, the understanding and avoidance of epidemics in livestock is a major focus of interest in the control of zoonosis, given how common it is for a disease to jump to humans. Consequently, researchers started using network science and population dynamics to understand the patterns of livestock trade movements and disease spread dynamics. Many works have been published after the FMD outbreak of 2001 when issues related to the management and control of infectious diseases in livestock were raised [1, 3, 4]. These initial works employed a network approach that traces the transmission of the disease using the contacts between livestock locations. The result of these works was the understanding of the structure of animal contacts as the main culprit of fast spreads.

After 2005, the use of the techniques from network science became more commonplace, with many works making use of open datasets of livestock movement [2, 5, 7, 9, 11]. Generally, the papers agreed with the fact that movement and the contacts are the main reasons for disease spread in livestock, especially cattle. As cattle production continues to grow, particularly in underdeveloped nations, it becomes necessary to understand the characteristics of livestock contact networks under the conditions of production in those countries. Most of the work done thus far looks at datasets in countries where the conditions for production are ideal, and the tracing is near-perfect. As a result, we observe an imbalance between the regions with large productions and the datasets studied (see Fig. 2). Most of the works are related to European datasets because of availability of data in these countries. Yet, many of the largest beef producers in the world (and hence the locations with the largest datasets) have not being studied well enough. Furthermore, in some of these locations the tracking technology is not the state-of-the-art or local conditions make it hard to employ the state-of-the-art.

The economic pressures in poorer nations coupled with the poor tracking infrastructure makes it easier for people to trade cattle without reporting it, that is, the official datasets probably fail to capture the reality. Therefore, it is likely that the collected data missing information which can affect the level of risk to epidemics in those areas. The missing information can include inaccuracies regarding the exact number of livestock traded, transactions that happen but are not recorded, and lack of reporting for certain premises.

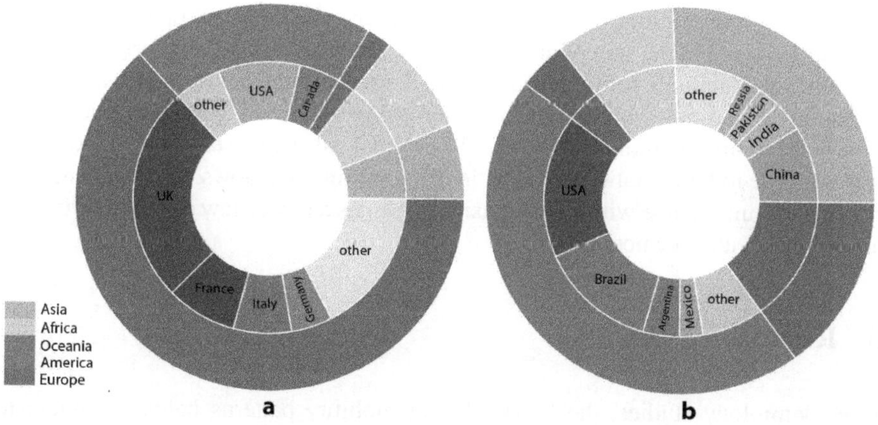

Fig. 2 Here we see **a** the number of papers related to cattle trade dataset of each continent in contrast with **b** the amount of beef production across the world). In order to estimate the number of publications that contain keywords cattle, network, and epidemic, and variations of it, we counted the publications between years 2001 to 2019 appearing in the Arxiv[2], Web of Science[3], and Scopus[4]

[2] https://arxiv.org (last accessed: 26 May 2020).

[3] https://webofknowledge.com (last accessed: 26 May 2020).

[4] https://scopus.com (last accessed: 26 May 2020).

Take Brazil as an example. There are 213.5 million heads[5] of bovine livestock reported in 2021 and the tracking of these animals is done manually [10]. Within Brazil, the state of Minas Gerais ranks third in number of bovine livestock, with almost 22.02 million heads; our work here deals with a large dataset from this state collected from 2013–2016.

2 Data and Methods

In this work, we use a dataset related to cattle movement from the state of Minas Gerais in Brazil. Minas Gerais is the fourth-largest state in the country (approximately 586.5 million km^2) and the one with the most number of cities: 853 as of 2019. In Minas Gerais, cattle trade data has been recorded by the Institute of Agriculture (IMA) for the period of 2013–2016. In this study, we investigate 6 months of this period, from January to June 2013, representing all the types of activities related to trading and movement of cattle. 6 months of data contains 139,681 premises (in 853 cities) which are involved in 510,747 transactions (trades) of 8,709,954 animals.

Cattle trade can be represented in terms of a network where nodes correspond to premises, and a directed edge exists between two nodes if a movement of cattle occurs in that direction between the corresponding premises. This network can be weighted by the number of transactions between two locations or the number of animals involved in the sum of all transactions. In this work, our network is based on the number of animals being traded. Due to the scale of the dataset, this paper focus on the investigation of missing information using a network generated with trades took place in first six months of 2013. The original dataset presents daily records. So it is possible to build static snapshots in different time windows Δt. The generated network is quite sparse with a low density, but it has a power-law degree distribution as found in scale-free networks.

3 Results

In epidemiology studies, the knowledge of mobility patterns helps us anticipate possible behaviours that an epidemic could exhibit. When contacts and mobility patterns are represented using a network and the data is collected manually, there is always a chance that the representation is flawed due to missing links and nodes arising from unobserved contact points.

The modelling of missing information has a direct effect on epidemic behaviour estimation. The network may exhibit different behaviour to the exposure to infection under uncertainty. We model 3 scenarios. *(1)* Uncertainty in the number of animals being traded, thus affecting the weights of the edges; we assume underreporting, meaning that the weight of edges in the network is a lower bound. *(2)* Similar to the

[5] https://www.statista.com (last accessed: 26 Jan 2022).

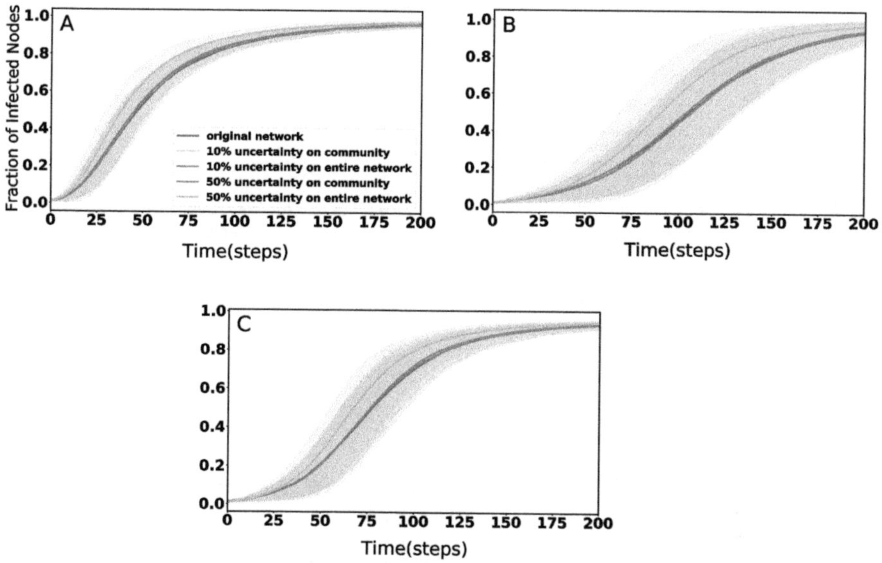

Fig. 3 Uncertainty in the number of animals traded (Scenario 1). Illustration of epidemic using SI model with $\beta = 0.001$ in synthetic networks **A** Barabási-Albert, **B** Watts-Strogatz, **C** Erdös-Rényi. Two cases of uncertainty are considered: *(1)* an increase in the value of the weight of edges in the entire network, *(2)* an increase in the weight of edges in the largest community of the network in terms of the number of nodes. For each case, we run two levels of uncertainty: a variation of up to 10% of edge weights, and up to 50%. The transmission rate is selected as small as 0.001 in order to achieve a distinguishable probability of infection transmission for different weights of edges. We generate synthetic networks by using the following parameters. There are 500 nodes in each network. Barabási-Albert algorithm generates a network in which new nodes with two edges are preferentially attached to existing nodes with high degrees. The connection probability of each pair of nodes in Erdös-Rényi network is 0.008. In Watts-Strogatz network, each node is connected to its four nearest neighbours in a ring topology, and rewiring happens with a probability of 0.5

first scenario, the underreporting could lead to relationships being created that did not exist previously; we treat this differently because it affects the connectivity of the network more directly than the first scenario. *(3)* Last, we look at the possibility of "rouge" locations which were not part of the network but actually exist. The evaluation of this scenario in the network requires adding new nodes to the original network. Growing a network should be done in a way that maintains its overall characteristics unchanged. In this paper, we have been careful to implement a method which respect the specific features of each type of network used.

We evaluate the three uncertainty scenarios argued above using simulations in synthetic networks before dealing with real networks. This approach allows us to understand the effect of uncertainty on the topology and dynamics in networks where characteristics are already known in the literature (Figs. 3, 4 and 5). In order to generate these synthetic networks, we generate them at the same density as the network derive from the MG dataset.

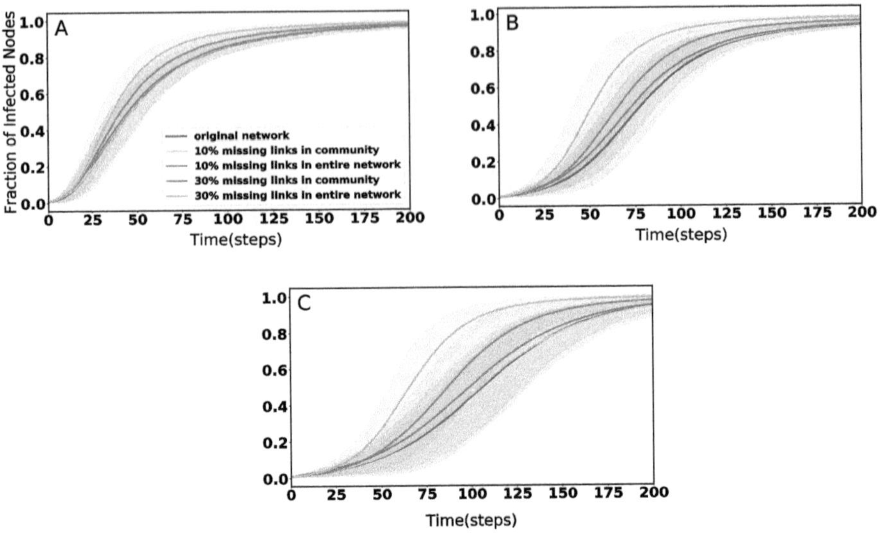

Fig. 4 Uncertainty regarding the existence of links (Scenario 2). Illustration of epidemic using SI model with $\beta = 0.001$ in synthetic networks **A** Barabási-Albert, **B** Watts-Strogatz, **C** Erdös-Rényi. The lines show the epidemic behaviour in the networks. Two cases are considered for adding missing links. The first adds a certain number of links (a percentage of the total number of edges) to the entire network. The second adds a certain number of links (a percentage of the number of edges between nodes within largest community) to the largest community of the network. For each case, we run two levels of uncertainty, with 10 and 30% of edges added. The weights of edges (the original and newly added) in synthetic networks are based on the distribution of the number of animals traded in the cattle trade dataset

In the simulations, we look at the effect of locality by having the issues (missing information) implemented globally and locally. In the real networks we have well-defined regions within the state and that is used for the concept of local, in the synthetic network we use the idea of community to look at local uncertainty. The spread of a hypothetical disease along the nodes of the network is simulated using a Susceptible-Infected (SI) model.

Figure 3 shows the differences in weights do not significantly change the epidemic behaviour except when the uncertainty is very high in most contacts, which we deem to be unrealistic and used here just for illustration. It is unlikely that a dataset would have 50% of the number of animals being incorrect. In Fig. 4, networks with 10% of missing links, even locally, start to behave differently from the original network, showing that missing links can be more damaging than wrong information about the weight of the links. In the case of missing nodes, the situation is exacerbated, showing that the existence of unreported locations can lead to significant changes in the epidemic behaviour (Fig. 5). The case of missing nodes is more dangerous because as they are added, they are more likely to change the connectivity level of the network.

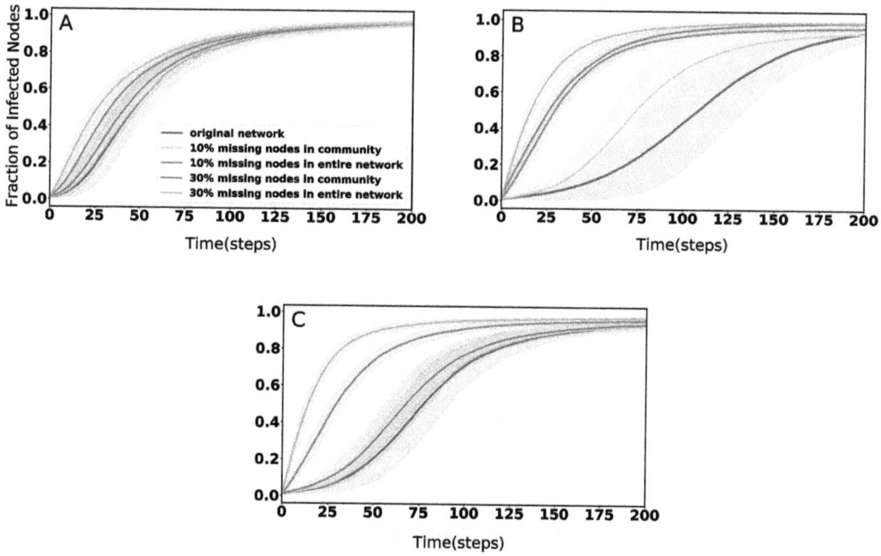

Fig. 5 Uncertainty regarding the existence of unknown nodes (Scenario 3). Illustration of epidemic using SI model with $\beta = 0.001$ in synthetic networks **A** Barabási-Albert, **B** Watts-Strogatz, **C** Erdös-Rényi. The lines show the epidemic behaviour in the networks. Two cases are considered for adding missing nodes. The first one adds a certain number of nodes (a percentage of the total number of nodes) to the entire network. The second one adds a certain number of nodes (a percentage of the number of nodes in largest community) to the largest community of the network. For each case, we run two levels of uncertainty, with 10 and 30% of nodes added

Recall that this paper uses a dataset related to the cattle movements from January to June 2013 in the State of Minas Gerais (MG). We generated a network of premises which has characteristics of a Barabási-Albert network. The state of Minas Geraes has been divided into 5 regions (North, East, Center, West, and South) which we use in the charts for looking at the local uncertainty. For each of the three uncertainty scenarios, we test the effect of locality with the East and West, but in Fig. 9 we look at all regions; this figure also has a map of Minas Gerais showing the 5 regions.

Figure 6 depicts the scenario of uncertainty regarding the number of animals being traded–the weight of the links in the network. The results are similar to what we had for synthetic networks, meaning that there is no significant difference on the epidemic curve when the only aspect that is inaccurate is the number of animals traded. There is a slight difference on the behaviour when the uncertainty is on the entire network at a high value (about 50% of the value declared). Given such inaccuracies are unlikely to exist, we deem that uncertainty in number of animals traded not to be of concern.

The missing links in the network appear when there are unregistered transactions between locations that have never traded according to the official dataset. It can be seen from Fig. 7 that the number of infected places is significantly higher than that in the network without missing links. For both 10 and 30% of missing links, the behaviour of the epidemic is different, for the case of the entire network and the case

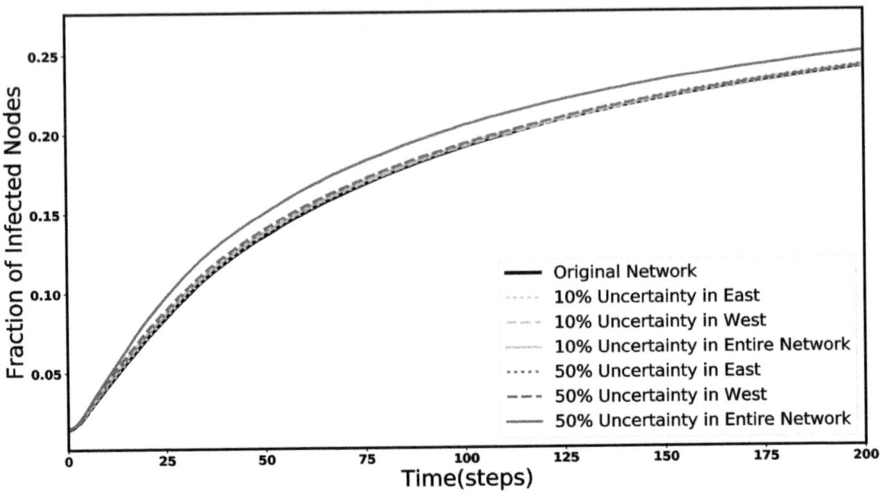

Fig. 6 Epidemic in the network with uncertain numbers of animals being traded (Scenario 1). The SI model is used with $\beta = 0.001$ (transmission rate). Uncertainty on the number of animals being traded can take place between two premises that are already connected in the network. In order to add uncertainty, three cases are considered: *(1)* an increase in the value of the weight of edges in the entire network, *(2)* an increase in the weight of edges in the east region, *(3)* an increase in the weight of edges in the west region. For each case, we run two levels of uncertainty: a variation of up to 10% of edge weights, and up to 50%

for the both regions with the largest and smallest number of transactions (East and West).

The case of missing nodes arises when a premise has transactions, but has not been registered as an active contact place in the dataset. The unregistered contact points are simulated by adding a certain number of missing nodes to the network locally or globally. Newly added nodes are assigned degrees using the degree distribution of the original network. New nodes are connected to the original network in a way consistent with real transactions; since there are more transactions between premises in the same region, there are more intra-regional transactions than inter-regional transactions. Probabilities of inter-regional and intra-regional transactions are calculated for a given region based on its fraction of real transactions. The case of missing nodes is the most significant one in terms of the epidemic, as shown in Fig. 8.

Movement along the edges of the network provides a major source of contact between populations of animals in the premises, which are the origin and destination of the movement. We can model untracked patterns more realistically by identifying high-risk spatial parts in real networks. A high-risk location is one that gets infected faster and has a higher percentage of cases of infection.

Following the characterisation of the cattle network, the SI model is applied to the network to assess the epidemic risk if a particular area of MG becomes a superspreader, meaning all cattle within that area are infected. The MG is divided into five regions (Fig. 9a). Risk is determined by the number of infected cases in

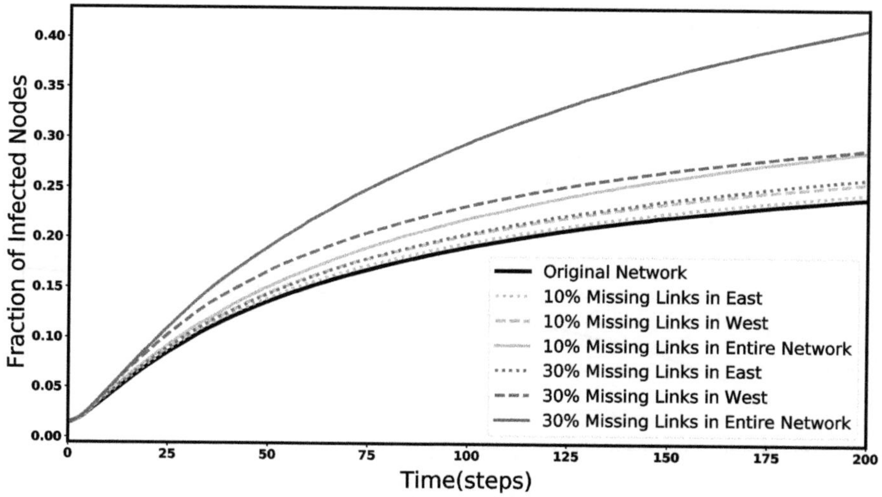

Fig. 7 Epidemic in the network loading under uncertainty regarding the existence of links (Scenario 2). We use a SI model with $\beta = 0.001$. It is assumed that unrecorded transactions could occur between two properties that have never been traded before. In order to add missing links, two cases are considered. The first is to add a certain number of links (a percentage of the total number of edges) to the entire network. The second method is to add missing links within a particular region (we focused on east and west). In this case, the number of new added edges are based on a percentage of the number of edges between nodes in the region. Each case is tested twice with the following percentages: (1) 10% (2) 30%. The weights of the newly added edges are chosen from the distribution of the weights in the original network

each region, which depends on the location of that region and the structure of cattle movements in that region. Figure 9a shows the number of infected cases per region for three types of networks. The first is a network with no uncertainty. Next are two networks with uncertainty. On networks, an infection process is simulated in which one of the other regions is assumed to be infected at the beginning. According to our results, western part of the country is always more affected, regardless of the region where the outbreak began. Hence, taking into account the number of infected cases interpreted as a risk related to each region, the west as the most risky region. In contrast, the east is regarded as the safest.

According to Fig. 9a outbreaks do not infect the regions in their entirety. At the end of the infection process when the number of infected cases does not change anymore, the final number of infected premises indicates the saturation point for each region. The saturation points also indicate that there is a percentage of premises that are safe from contagion. Note that in Fig. 9a we use a network build from 31 days of transactions. It then begs the question regarding the effect of the number of days considered in the network and whether the saturation points changes.

Figure 9b shows the mean of the saturation point values in each region of the network without uncertainty. The x-axis represents the size of the network, i.e. the number of days used to generate the network, ranging from one day (the first day of

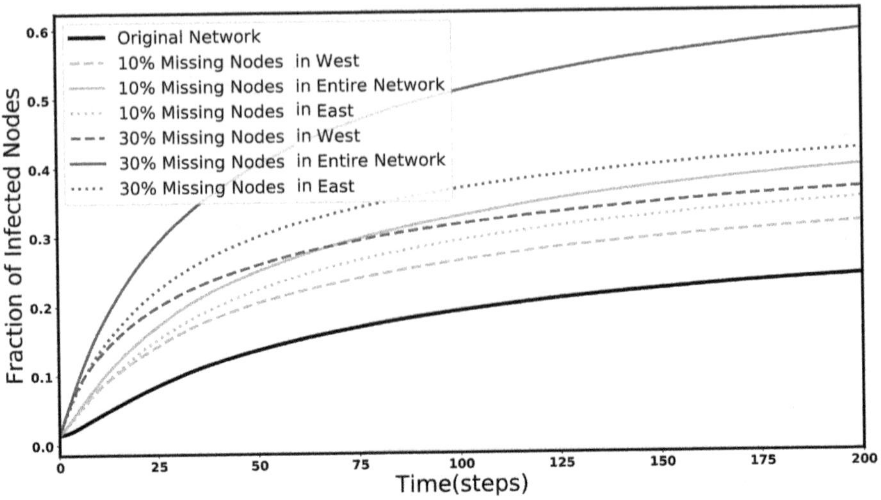

Fig. 8 Epidemic in the network loading under uncertainty regarding the existence of unknown nodes (Scenario 3). We use a SI model with $\beta = 0.001$. These missing places are considered initially infected in our simulation. In order to add missing nodes, two cases are considered. The first is to add a certain number of nodes (a percentage of the total number of nodes) to the entire network. Secondly, we add missing nodes within a particular region (east and west). A percentage of the number of nodes in the region is used for the number of new nodes added. Cases are tested with the following percentages: (1) 10% (2) 30%

the year 2013) to 100 days (the 100th day of the year 2013). Note that the figure does appear to show that the size of the network becomes less important as the number of days considered increases, meaning that regardless of the size of the network, some premises are not infected.

We simulate the Susceptible-Infected-Recovered (SIR) model on our cattle trade network, since the SI model does not allow the analysis of epidemic thresholds [6]. During an outbreak, the infected animals will be killed, so the R compartment contains removed cases. Here, we examine a simulated SIR spreading process in order to predict the epidemic threshold for the networks loading under uncertainty. As Fig. 10 illustrates, there is not significant difference between network without uncertainty and network loading under change in weight of edges. The range of β includes common values for real cattle diseases. The killing of an infected animal can be abstracted in network terms as a change in edge weight. Figure 10 indicates that altering the weight of edges in a network will not affect the spread of diseases (something that we have also observed in synthetic networks). Additionally, it suggests that killing infected animals and trading the rest of the herd is ineffective in preventing the spread of disease.

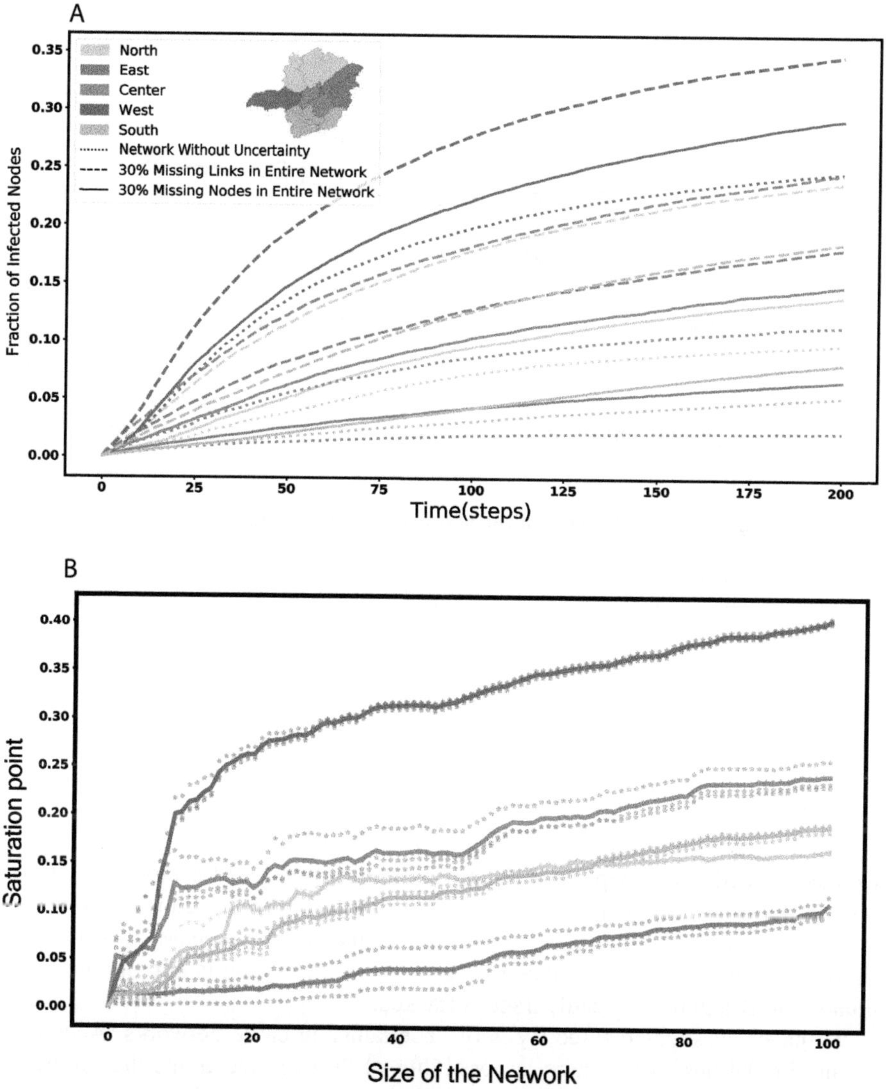

Fig. 9 A Mean fraction of the infected cases in a given region. Every region undergoes infection for four runs, during each run one of the other regions is the initially-infected zone. Calculations are done in network with no uncertainty (dashed lines), network with 30% missing links added to network (dotted lines), and network with 30% missing nodes added to network (solid lines). **B Saturation point.** When we run an epidemic model, the speed of the contamination slows down with time. Because the simulation is measured for each region, with the other 4 regions being the infected region, we could have different behaviours. As can be seen from (**A**), the outbreak could not contaminate all premises for a network of a given size. Thus, the final number of infected premises could indicate a saturation point for each region. in (**B**) we see the solid line as the average of the 4 runs. We can observe again here that the west is the most vulnerable, while the east is the most robust. The robustness may come from the fact that the east may not be as well-connected to the rest of the network. The size of the network is controlled by the number of days considered when building the network

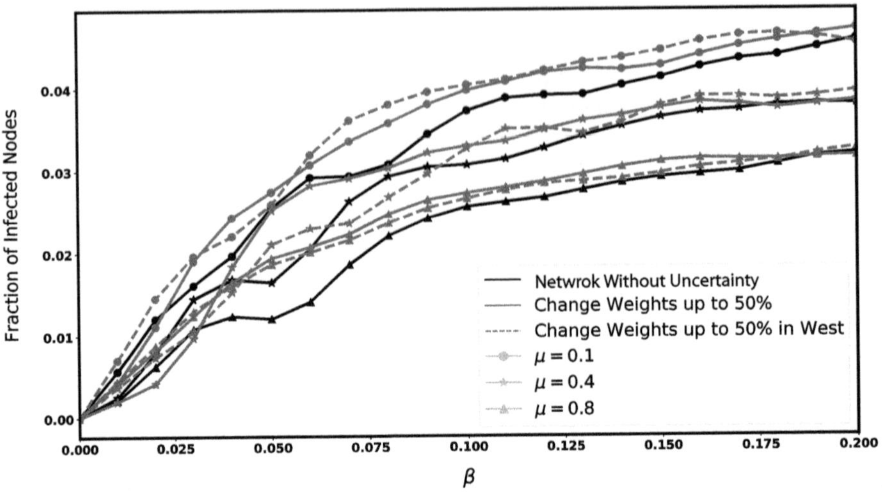

Fig. 10 Simulation of a SIR model in the network of Minas Gerais. The fraction of infected nodes is illustrated with respect to transmission rate (β) values. The model simulated in network without uncertainty and networks with uncertainty in the number of animals traded (Scenario 1). Solid green lines refers to the network with 50% is added to the weights in the entire network. Dashed green lines are related to the network that up to 50% is added to the weights in the west. Different markers show different values of recovery rates as follows: triangle: $\mu = 0.8$, star: $\mu = 0.4$, circle: $\mu = 0.1$. In this process, the infection spreads through five steps. During each step, each node can transmit the disease to all of its neighbours and then have a chance to recover

4 Conclusion

We have argued in this paper that the process of disease spread is closely related to patterns of contact between individuals. This pattern could change the behaviour we expect from the epidemic based on the level of uncertainty we have. It is therefore important to find a way to evaluate uncertainty in a way that is appropriate to the situation in Brazil of how cattle trade is tracked.

We have investigated three types of uncertainty in cattle networks. According to our simulations, when there is possibility of "rouge" locations, the difference in the number of infected cases compared to the network without uncertainty is the greatest. Another key aspect relates to the spatial distribution of uncertainties. By recognising high-risk spatial parts in real networks, we can model untracked patterns more realistically. During an epidemic in Minas Gerais, the West represents the highest risk. Based on our epidemic threshold analysis, it is clear that killing the infected animals and keeping trading open is not an effective way to reduce the outbreak size. Using partial interventions, such as focusing on separate regions and targeting inter-regional trades, could mitigate the effects of an outbreak. A possible solution is to decrease the trades in high-risk regions. Another option is to restrict the transactions between high-risk and low-risk areas.

The results of cattle studies can aid the monitoring system in finding dangerous regions. The areas that face a critical situation in an outbreak and become a superspreader when there is a pandemic.

References

1. Bates, T.W., Thurmond, M.C., Carpenter, T.E.: Description of an epidemic simulation model for use in evaluating strategies to control an outbreak of foot-and-mouth disease. Am. J. Vet. Res. **64**(2), 195–204 (2003)
2. Bigras-Poulin, M., Thompson, R., Chriél, M., Mortensen, S., Greiner, M.: Network analysis of danish cattle industry trade patterns as an evaluation of risk potential for disease spread. Prev. Vet. Med. **76**(1–2), 11–39 (2006)
3. Ferguson, N.M., Donnelly, C.A., Anderson, R.M.: The foot-and-mouth epidemic in great britain: pattern of spread and impact of interventions. Science **292**(5519), 1155–1160 (2001)
4. Gibbens, J., Wilesmith, J.: Temporal and geographical distribution of cases of foot-and-mouth disease during the early weeks of the 2001 epidemic in great britain. Vet. Rec. **151**(14), 407–412 (2002)
5. Kiss, I.Z., Green, D.M., Kao, R.R.: The network of sheep movements within great britain: network properties and their implications for infectious disease spread. J. R. Soc. Interface **3**(10), 669–677 (2006)
6. Mei, W., Mohagheghi, S., Zampieri, S., Bullo, F.: On the dynamics of deterministic epidemic propagation over networks. Annu. Rev. Control. **44**, 116–128 (2017)
7. Ortiz-Pelaez, A., Pfeiffer, D., Soares-Magalhaes, R., Guitian, F.: Use of social network analysis to characterize the pattern of animal movements in the initial phases of the 2001 foot and mouth disease (fmd) epidemic in the uk. Prev. Vet. Med. **76**(1–2), 40–55 (2006)
8. Sharpley, R., Craven, B.: The 2001 foot and mouth crisis-rural economy and tourism policy implications: a comment. Curr. Issues Tour. **4**(6), 527–537 (2001)
9. Shirley, M., Rushton, S.: Where diseases and networks collide: lessons to be learnt from a study of the 2001 foot-and-mouth disease epidemic. Epidemiol. Infect. **133**(6), 1023–1032 (2005)
10. Sourcing, P.R., Briefings, P.: Socio-environmental monitoring of the cattle sector in Brazil. Tech. rep, Proforest (2017)
11. Webb, C.R.: Farm animal networks: unraveling the contact structure of the british sheep population. Prev. Vet. Med. **68**(1), 3–17 (2005)

Building a Reliable, Dynamic and Temporal Synthetic Model of the World Trade Web

Sean Kennedy, Michael Wish, Philip Smith, James Sherrell, William Shields, and Ralucca Gera

Abstract This paper presents an accurate, scalable, time-dependent synthetic network model for the World Trade Web (WTW), whose nodes are the different countries that traded from 1996–2020. Using only an initial distribution of countries' global Gross Domestic Product (GDP) as an input, our synthetic network model initializes weighted undirected edges corresponding to total trade between two countries using the presence of a hidden fitness variable dependent on GDP. The synthetic model simulates the creation and deletion of new and existing trade relationships aligned with real-world data. Our results show that this simulated network continues to faithfully approximate the data from WTW about 20 years after creation within a reasonable degree of accuracy.

1 Introduction and Motivation

Massive global trade disruptions have persisted since the beginning of the COVID-19 pandemic. Impediments to everyday life have been commonplace, and unforeseen shortages in goods have stressed traditional supply chains. Accurate, scalable, and interpretable models are essential for mitigating future disruptions to global supply chains. An accurate approximation of real data through synthetic networks could provide extraordinary results in the form of data for simulations, analysis of correlations between factors, or predictive models. So long as we capture the underlying features of our real-world data, synthetic networks are computationally cheap to produce,

S. Kennedy
Department of Electrical and Computer Engineering, Naval Postgraduate School, Monterey, CA, USA

M. Wish
Department of Physics, Naval Postgraduate School, Monterey, CA, USA

P. Smith · J. Sherrell · R. Gera (✉)
Department of Applied Mathematics, Naval Postgraduate School, Monterey, CA, USA
e-mail: rgera@nps.edu

W. Shields
Department of Operations Research, Naval Postgraduate School, Monterey, CA, USA

D. Pacheco et al. (eds.), *Complex Networks XIII*, Springer Proceedings in Complexity,
https://doi.org/10.1007/978-3-031-17658-6_6

easily scalable and may reduce bias when constructed to mimic desired properties of the real data.

Thus, in this research we develop a synthetic network generator that closely approximates the real-world World Trade Web (WTW) using gross domestic product (GDP) as an input. We will then create sample networks and compare our time-series synthetic model against the WTW using key network metrics.

In the future, we envision our model being subject to a series of different attacks or natural changes in attempts to simulate real-world disruptions, including both regional and global events. If this synthetic network model reacts similarly to real-world trade disruptions, a synthetic network model generator could be used in the future to plan for and mitigate disruptions in the WTW.

We use UN data [3] to create a weighted, directed temporal network [9], where each time slice of the network represents a year's worth of imports and exports in billions of US dollars for 190 countries. This temporal network represents world trade data from 1996 to 2020. All traded goods are considered and valued in 2022 US dollars. We also acquired world GDP data from the same timeframe from the World Bank [13].

2 Related Work

Interactions in many technological, biological, and social fields have been modeled as complex networks [11]. Econometrics is an especially interesting field where networks can provide additional explanatory power for both individual behavior and aggregate outcomes [4]. Of specific interest are the properties of individual nodes within a network that affect the probability of forming additional connections [1]. While the traditional "rich get richer" approach from the Barabási-Albert synthetic network model works well for network growth, we seek improved modeling for networks with specific interactions, such as the WTW.

Connecting two vertices in a relatively scale-free environment when the bidirectional edge creates a mutual benefit is a standard interaction model [2]. In this model, each node from the N node choices is assigned some fitness parameter, taken from a distribution $\rho(x)$. That is, for every pair of vertices (i, j), an edge is drawn with probability $f(x_i, x_j)$. If f is constant for all nodes pairs, this will produce a standard Erdős-Rényi Model, but a more dynamic probability function will produce a more scale-free model [5].

These fitness-based models have been successfully used to model the World Trade Web in both directed and undirected network models using unweighted edges [6, 8]. That is, we create a network whose nodes are the countries in a given data set, say N countries, and edges are added by using hidden fitness variable x_i proportional to i^{th} country's GDP: the probability that an edge between countries is added i and j $(1 \leq i \neq j \leq N)$ modeled as

$$P_L[x_i, x_j] = \frac{\alpha_0 x_i x_j}{1 + \beta_0 x_i x_j}, \tag{1}$$

where α_0 and β_0 are free parameters of the model input [6]. From this probability, we can compute the expected number of links, L_{exp} as

$$L_{exp} = \sum_{i \neq j} P_L[x_i, x_j]. \tag{2}$$

This metric is used for comparison between real and synthetic results in Sect. 4 [8].

Due to the nature of the WTW, it is not necessary to expand a model to the directed case. After the collapse of the USSR, the number of countries has only increased slowly, while the number of trade relationships has increased significantly faster, visible as the WTW network becomes denser and denser. If we were to analyze the WTW in its directed form, we would see mutually directed edges between countries becoming more and more common as time goes on. Eventually, if node i was connected to node j in the directed network, node j would be connected to node i with a high probability. Thus, it becomes feasible to view this directed network as an undirected network, with a low probability p that each individual bidirectional edge be replaced with a directional edge in an arbitrary direction [7]. While there is some loss of information in reduction to a unidirectional network, important trade values can be recovered [8].

In order to maintain a consistent model across years, our network must be a temporal network in which each time slice represents each year of the data set. Many temporal networks have additional constraints, but since the WTW is mainly an industrial and infrastructural network, most dynamic concepts such as latency and efficiencies may probably be safely ignored [9].

3 Methodology

Our methodology for creating time-varying, weighted synthetic WTW networks is based on existing methods for generating static instances of unweighted synthetic WTW networks. Previous research identified that the existence of trade relationships between countries is strongly dependent on the relative sizes of the countries' GDPs [6, 8]. This insight was used to develop a method for synthetic WTW generation that takes in country GDP data as an input, and provides an unweighted, undirected network as an output. The resulting unweighted, undirected network possesses a degree distribution approximating the real-world WTW when the corresponding real-world GDP data is provided as input [6, 8]. Our work extends this method through: (1) random generation of appropriate edge weights representing total annual trade between each connected country pair and (2) implementation of a time-based evolution to the synthetic WTW network in which edges with large trade weights are preferentially maintained, edges with smaller trade weights may disappear, and new edges may be created. We incorporate these additional phenomena into our model to provide coherence between each year's model output, which better matches real-world data. While these phenomena may be ascribable to various complex economic or geopolitical mechanisms (e.g., "Globalization"), the development of our model sets aside such underlying mechanisms in favor of heuristically determined factors based on the trade data itself.

The following is a high-level summary of our iterative model. First, we use provided GDP data to create an initial random network based on the methodology of [6]. Then, we assign weights to each edge in the initial network using a heuristic distribution based on each country's GDP. This step completes the initialization of our WTW synthetic network as the first year's network output. Each subsequent year's output is generated from the previous year's output by (1) randomly adding more weighted edges where none currently exist (as a function of the GDP of the two potential countries to be connected), (2) deleting a random portion of existing trade edges according to a heuristically determined distribution, and (3) adjusting trade values for maintained edges based on changes in the associated countries' GDPs. The details of the model are provided in the subsections below.

3.1 Data Acquisition and Cleaning

We obtained our reference WTW data set from the United Nations (UN) Comtrade Database from 1996 through 2020 [3]. We formed a temporal, undirected network from this data, with each year as a time-step. A country's interaction with another country in a given year was modeled as an edge in that time-step, with an edge weight of the total dollar amount of trade in both directions.

Some data cleaning was necessary. Several countries had no trade for specific years, indicating either years in which that country reported nothing to the UN or errors in UN data compilation. To avoid issues in our data analysis that such errors would bring forth, we removed all countries whose trade disappeared for at least one year from the data set. Combined, these countries amounted to a small proportion of our data set, and thus their removal is unlikely to affect the underlying traits of the data.

We also gathered GDP data from the World Bank website [13]. Like the UN trade data, GDP data was not always consistent, with several countries lacking GDP data in certain years. These countries with inconsistent GDP data were likewise removed from our analysis. In total, there were 162 countries that had consistent GDP and trade data for the years 1996 through 2020. It is from this data set that we determined the global parameters for our time-varying synthetic WTW model.

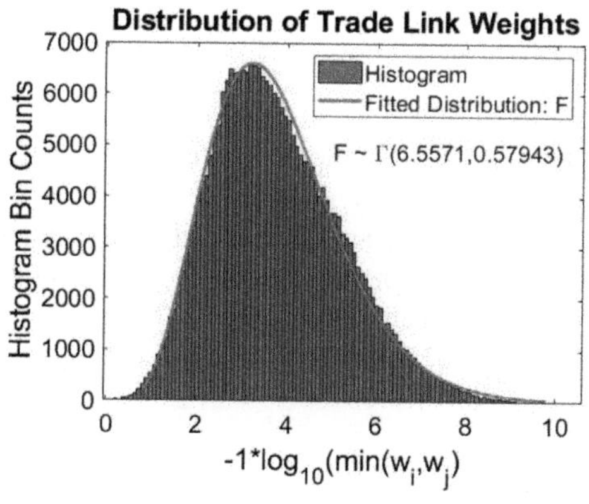

Fig. 1 Reversed distribution of relative trade edge weights in 1996-2020 data, overlaid with fitted Gamma distribution. Analysis and figure creation performed in MATLAB

3.2 *Synthetic Network: Initialization*

We initialize the synthetic WTW model using the method of [6]: taking w_i $(i = 1, \ldots, N)$, as the GDP of the i-th country in the initial year, we first normalize each country's GDP by the mean GDP to obtain each country's so-called "fitness score" x_i as

$$x_i \equiv \frac{w_i}{\sum_{i=1}^{N} w_i / N}. \tag{3}$$

Next, we consider adding edges by looking at each pair of countries. We randomly generate undirected, unweighted edges between the pair, where the probability of an edge existing between each pair is computed via (1) [6].

To create realistic weights for these generated edges, we use a heuristic from the distribution of relative edge weights in the cleaned 1996–2020 trade data. From this data, we found that the distribution of the fraction of the smaller of the two country's GDPs very closely follows a reversed log-gamma distribution, as can be seen in Fig. 1.

Thus, we generate random edge weights, e_{ij}, according to the following formula:

$$e_{ij} = 10^{-F} \cdot \min(w_i, w_j), \tag{4}$$

where $F \sim \Gamma(6.5571, 0.5794)$. This method of generating random edge weights has the benefit of always being a positive fraction of the smaller of the two countries GDP's, and avoids unrealistic scenarios where one country's trade is several orders of magnitude larger than its nominal GDP.

The creation of network edges and associated weights in the initial year completes the initialization step of the model. The weighted adjacency matrix that is derived from this network is the model's output for the initial year.

3.3 Synthetic Network Growth: Subsequent Years

We generate each subsequent year in the model's output from the previous year's output along with updated GDP data for each country. In a single-pass through the current adjacency matrix, we check the trade relationship status for each pair of countries, with action then taken dependent on this status as follows. If the two countries do not currently have a trade relationship, then an edge is created between them with probability:

$$P_L[x_i, x_j] = \frac{\alpha x_i x_j}{1 + \beta x_i x_j}, \tag{5}$$

where x_i, x_j, and P_L have the meaning of the initialization step's variables, albeit with current year GDP values. The free parameters α and β are allowed to differ from the initialization parameters α_0 and β_0 as discussed in Sect. 4. Weights are likewise assigned to any newly created edges using (4) with the current year's GDP values.

If a trade relationship (i.e. weighted edge) already exists for the country pair under inspection, the edge is subjected to random deletion. The probability of edge deletion, P_D, is a function of the current edge weight and the two countries' respective GDPs:

$$y \equiv \log_{10}\left(\frac{e_{ij}}{w_i + w_j}\right), \tag{6}$$

$$P_D[x_i, x_j] = \begin{cases} 10^{(ay^2+by+c)}, & \text{if } y \geq 10^{-10} \\ 0.36, & \text{otherwise.} \end{cases} \tag{7}$$

We heuristically determine the parameters $a = -0.0483$, $b = -0.961$, $c = -5.223$, and the general shape of (7) from the 1996-2020 trade data. First, we compute overlapping histograms of the different years showing the count of trade relationships that are maintained versus trade relationships which are terminated in a year-over-year fashion, stratified by the value of y from (6). We then plot the ratio of bin counts as a function of y, and determine that these values follow a roughly quadratic curve in the log-space of these ratios.

Fitting a curve to the logarithm of the 10th through 30th bins yields the heuristic for $y > 10^{-10}$ in (7), summarized graphically in Fig. 2. Note that only the 10th through 30th bins were used since the other bins had too few instances of trade continuing or stopping for the ratio to be statistically meaningful. These 10th through 30th bins roughly correspond with the range of orange bins which are visible in the top portion of Fig. 2. For values of $y < 10^{-10}$, we simply set the the probability equal to the maximum of the fitted curve, which is approximately 0.36 in the second plot of Fig. 2.

If a trade relationship already exists for the country pair under inspection, and it is not identified for deletion, the weight is slightly adjusted to account for year-over-year changes in the GDPs of the associated countries. We define the relative change in GDP between countries i and j, r_{ij}, as:

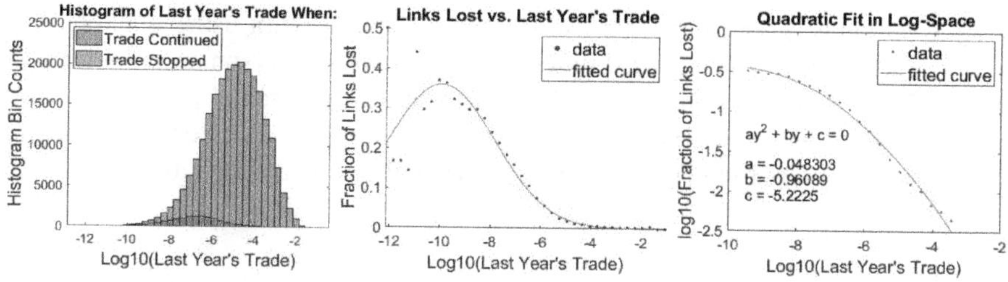

Fig. 2 Left: Histogram of previous year's relative trade value when trade continued and when trade stopped. Middle: Fraction of edges lost taken by computing ratio of histogram bin counts from left image. Right: Log-space of fraction of edges lost for the 10th through 30th bins in the histogram at left, along with fitted quadratic curve. Figures and quadratic fit were generated using MATLAB

$$r_{ij} = \frac{(\min(w_i(y), w_j(y)) - \min(w_i(y-1), w_j(y-1))}{\min(w_i(y-1), w_j(y-1))}, \tag{8}$$

where $w_i(y)$ is the GDP of country i in the current year y, and $w_i(y-1)$ is the GDP of country i in the previous year. If $r_{ij} > 5\%$, then the current edge weight, e_{ij}, is increased by a factor uniformly drawn from the range $[1, 1 + 2r_{ij}]$. If $r_{ij} < -5\%$, then e_{ij} is decreased by a factor uniformly drawn from the range $[1 + 2r_{ij}, 1]$. Otherwise, the change in GDP is relatively minor, and so the weight is adjusted by a factor uniformly drawn from the range [0.95, 1.05]. This effect is to increase trade weights when GDP growth allows, reduce trade weights when GDP shrinks, and randomly jitter trade weights when GDP remains relatively constant.

3.4 Algorithmic Performance

The synthetic model takes as input a matrix of GDP data of size $N \times M$, where each of the N rows represent individual countries, and each of the M columns represent years. The output of the synthetic model produces an $N \times N \times M$ data cube, where each $N \times N$ slice along the third dimension represents the weighted, symmetrical adjacency matrix for the WTW for a given year. In this sense, the output is the time-varying adjacency matrix of the graph representing the synthetic WTW.

The initialization and iterative loop are constructed such that each entry in the output matrix is computed exactly once. Since the computation of each entry is deterministic, the worst-case computation time for each entry of the output is a bounded constant. The overall algorithm thus possesses a worst-case time complexity of $O(N^2M)$. Since the initialization and iterative loop computations only require the current and previous year's state information, intermediate variables used in the algorithm have a space complexity bounded by the smaller of $O(N^2)$ and $O(NM)$. Since each of these bounds is smaller than the size of the $N \times N \times M$ output, the overall space complexity of the algorithm is also $O(N^2M)$.

As a reference point for future users, we ran the algorithm using our reference data set ($N = 162$, $M = 25$) 100 times on a Windows 10 personal computer with an i5-4670 (3.40 GHz) CPU and 32 GB of RAM. Chosen model parameters were $\alpha_0 = 220$, $\beta_0 = 80$, $\alpha = 200$, $\beta = 80$. The mean execution time for the algorithm with these inputs was found to be 0.519 seconds, with a standard deviation of 0.00907 seconds.

3.5 Connectivity Enforcement

The MATLAB implementation of the model was programmed supporting an option that requires all nodes to be connected during each time-step of the output. When selecting this option at the end of each time-step, the model merges two different components by randomly creating a bridge between two nodes in each component. The weight for the bridge is computed using (4). This merging processes is repeated until only a single connected component remains.

Given the iterative nature of this process, and the relatively expensive computation of the connected components during each iteration, this option has the potential to increase the run-time of the algorithm. However, we found that using parameter values of α_0, α, β_0, and β such that the synthetic WTW degree distribution approximates the real-world WTW distribution, there was no appreciable difference in actual execution time. This is due to the rarity of randomly obtaining multiple connected components when using the parameter values that approximate the real-world WTW.

4 Results and Analysis

We organize the analysis of our model into four parts: initial construction, GDP parameters, simulation parameters, and topological structure analysis.

4.1 Initial Construction

Our first attempt at creating the initialization of the model from the 1996 data yielded a smaller network characterized by a depressed degree distribution, especially among the high-degree nodes. This result is expected given that the edge construction probabilities at each time step, stemming from chosen constants α and β, are predicated on an existing representative network to add and remove edges. In the case of the base year however, the synthetic network is only constructed by adding edges to an empty graph of the appropriate order. Without data prior to the initial year, there are no existing edges to maintain, and so trade-link creation probabilities during initialization must be higher to compensate. To achieve this, we establish alternate values for α and β for model initialization. We refer to these parameters as α_0 and β_0.

Given the results from [6], we use the 1996 GDP distribution as the fitness variable to specify the apparent topological characteristics of the real network. We then obtain optimal values for α_0 and β_0 by minimizing the sum of the degree distribution error through the Nelder-Mead simplex algorithm [10]. While any network metrics might be optimized, we observe that reproducing the approximate degree distribution tends to align the other topological characteristics of the synthetic network with the real network. The values that optimize the degree distribution fit are $\alpha_0 = 220$ and $\beta_0 = 80$.

4.2 GDP Parameters

We generate realistic GDP data using parameters measured from the real-world GDP data. Using a log-normal distribution model for GDP data, we computed the mean and standard deviation of this log-normal distribution (in log terms) for each year of available data. The results are presented in Fig. 3. As shown, the base year has a mean of approximately 23.2 (approximately \$11.9B in nominal terms), and standard deviation of 2.46. The growth in the mean is approximately linear over the 25 year data set, and the standard deviation remains within a stable range between 2.35 and 2.47. Thus, we generate the base year's synthetic GDP data by randomly selecting values from the 1996 log-normal distribution for each country. Each subsequent

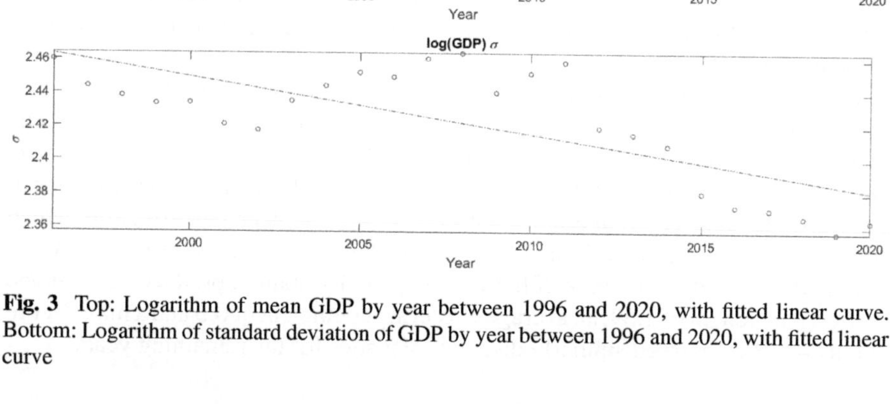

Fig. 3 Top: Logarithm of mean GDP by year between 1996 and 2020, with fitted linear curve. Bottom: Logarithm of standard deviation of GDP by year between 1996 and 2020, with fitted linear curve

year's GDP is generated by applying a random growth factor to the previous years' GDP value.

4.3 Simulation Parameters

Due to the randomness inherent in our method with respect to GDP parameters and edge weights, we simulated the synthetic WTW multiple times to avoid bias caused by statistical outliers. Using experimentally determined parameter values of $\alpha_0 = 200$ and $\beta_0 = 80$, we computed a running update of the mean and standard deviation of the parameters in Table 2 after each iteration. We found no significant changes occurred in the Table 2 entries after 30 iterations, and so the simulation was halted at that point.

4.4 Topological Structure Analysis

Tables 1 and 2 show statistics by year for the WTW network using real data and synthetic networks, respectively. We apply the initial construction parameters to 1996 and generate subsequent years iteratively via our methodology for adding and removing trade links. We average the synthetic network statistics of 30 simulations. Each row presents the statistics for each time slice of the temporal network, and global statistics are provided at the bottom of each table. As expected, the year-to-year comparison provides more meaningful data than the average data, where each network in our model is a time-dependent network stimulated by GDP growth and random processes.

The defining feature of the synthetic network is the annual increase in the number of edges that both approximates the actual growth in world trade links and preserves the remaining network topology. Many network characteristics are well-preserved, such as: average degree, average shortest path, average clustering coefficient, and the maximum k-core, with standard deviations as appropriate. We observe from Tables 1 and 2 that the synthetic network presents excellent approximations in each of the relevant statistics.

Figure 4 shows the real and synthetic degree distributions for each year.

We note that the synthetic data aligns well with the real data given the long time frame of the model. Note that the recreation of the degree distribution is not the sole indicator of a successful synthetic network. As a basis for comparison, we created a random MR-configuration graph for each year's actual degree distribution, which preserved none of the other desired topological characteristics. For example, an MR Configuration random network of the 1996 degree distribution produced an average shortest path length of 1.59, an average clustering coefficient of 0.5 and a max K-core of only 44. We observed similarly disparate statistics for the remaining years.

Table 1 Network statistics of the real WTW from 1996 to 2020

Year	N	E	Density	μ degree	σ degree	μ shortest path	σ shortest path	μ clustering coeff	σ clustering coeff	Max k-core
1996	162	7486	0.287	92.420	39.971	1.426	0.505	0.819	0.143	68
1997	162	7931	0.304	97.914	38.396	1.392	0.499	0.820	0.119	72
1998	162	8195	0.314	101.173	38.052	1.372	0.494	0.829	0.112	77
1999	162	8369	0.321	103.321	37.647	1.358	0.490	0.833	0.102	78
2000	162	9030	0.346	111.481	34.996	1.308	0.471	0.843	0.095	84
2001	162	9102	0.349	112.370	34.702	1.302	0.469	0.844	0.092	85
2002	162	9194	0.353	113.506	34.553	1.295	0.466	0.847	0.086	85
2003	162	9373	0.359	115.716	33.314	1.281	0.459	0.848	0.084	88
2004	162	9540	0.366	117.778	32.599	1.268	0.453	0.853	0.084	89
2005	162	9627	0.369	118.852	32.566	1.262	0.449	0.857	0.080	91
2006	162	9758	0.374	120.469	32.106	1.252	0.077	0.861	0.078	93
2007	162	9960	0.382	122.963	31.069	1.236	0.434	0.868	0.077	96
2008	162	9943	0.381	122.753	31.008	1.238	0.435	0.866	0.075	96
2009	162	10036	0.385	123.901	30.396	1.230	0.431	0.868	0.075	95
2010	162	10220	0.392	126.173	29.626	1.216	0.421	0.875	0.074	99
2011	162	10281	0.394	126.926	29.347	1.212	0.418	0.878	0.073	100
2012	162	10316	0.396	127.358	29.275	1.209	0.416	0.879	0.074	101
2013	162	10405	0.399	128.457	28.790	1.202	0.411	0.882	0.074	102
2014	162	10289	0.394	127.025	29.823	1.211	0.418	0.881	0.072	101
2015	162	10456	0.401	129.086	29.222	1.198	0.408	0.888	0.070	103
2016	162	10518	0.403	129.852	28.726	1.193	0.405	0.890	0.071	106
2017	162	10569	0.405	130.481	28.274	1.190	0.402	0.890	0.070	104
2018	162	10504	0.403	129.679	28.930	1.195	0.406	0.890	0.067	103
2019	162	10399	0.399	128.383	30.187	1.203	0.412	0.889	0.068	102
2020	162	9890	0.379	122.099	33.535	1.242	0.438	0.876	0.065	96
min		7486	0.287	92.420	28.274	1.190	0.402	0.819	0.065	68
max		10569	0.405	130.481	39.971	1.426	0.505	0.890	0.143	106
avg		9656	0.370	119.205	32.285	1.260	0.442	0.863	0.083	92.6
std		859.3	0.033	10.609	3.365	0.066	0.031	0.022	0.0181668	10.4

The tabulated statistics are derived from unweighted, undirected versions of the network. Due to the extremely high density of the network and the extremely high probability of reciprocal trade links, the topological characteristics of the weighted, directed networks persist in their simplified reductions [12]. However, we inspected several aspects of the weighted networks for verification and consistency. For example, in 1996, the total value of traded goods was \$999.3B out of a possible "world-

Table 2 Network statistics for our synthetic WTW computed over 30 iterations

Year	N	E	Density	μ Degree	σ Degree	μ Shortest Path	σ Shortest Path	μ Clustering Coeff	σ Clustering Coeff	Max k-Core
1996	162	7471	0.298	92.231	42.515	1.422	0.494	0.871	0.141	81
1997	162	7773	0.310	95.968	39.276	1.401	0.492	0.839	0.118	82
1998	162	8196	0.325	101.187	38.587	1.369	0.484	0.848	0.109	87
1999	162	8470	0.338	104.570	37.911	1.349	0.477	0.853	0.103	89
2000	162	8670	0.348	107.040	37.364	1.332	0.472	0.857	0.098	91
2001	162	8832	0.356	109.034	36.913	1.320	0.467	0.861	0.094	93
2002	162	8952	0.362	110.521	36.529	1.311	0.463	0.864	0.092	94
2003	162	9053	0.366	111.768	36.196	1.305	0.460	0.866	0.088	95
2004	162	9151	0.370	112.970	35.919	1.297	0.457	0.869	0.086	96
2005	162	9226	0.373	113.906	35.670	1.290	0.454	0.871	0.085	97
2006	162	9297	0.374	114.773	35.437	1.285	0.452	0.873	0.083	98
2007	162	9358	0.376	115.528	35.233	1.281	0.449	0.874	0.082	99
2008	162	9412	0.378	116.200	35.042	1.276	0.447	0.876	0.080	99
2009	162	9466	0.380	116.861	34.841	1.273	0.445	0.877	0.079	100
2010	162	9506	0.381	117.361	34.679	1.270	0.444	0.878	0.078	100
2011	162	9544	0.384	117.831	34.538	1.267	0.442	0.879	0.077	101
2012	162	9577	0.384	118.232	34.408	1.264	0.441	0.880	0.076	101
2013	162	9611	0.386	118.651	34.278	1.261	0.439	0.881	0.074	102
2014	162	9638	0.386	118.987	34.156	1.259	0.438	0.882	0.074	102
2015	162	9663	0.389	119.298	34.087	1.257	0.437	0.882	0.074	102
2016	162	9688	0.389	119.608	33.980	1.254	0.436	0.883	0.073	102
2017	162	9710	0.389	119.873	33.885	1.253	0.435	0.884	0.072	103
2018	162	9726	0.388	120.075	33.797	1.252	0.435	0.884	0.073	103
2019	162	9748	0.389	120.343	33.734	1.251	0.434	0.885	0.071	103
2020	162	9765	0.390	120.555	33.635	1.249	0.433	0.885	0.071	103
min		7471	0.298	92.231	33.635	1.249	0.433	0.839	0.071	81
max		9765	0.390	120.555	42.515	1.422	0.494	0.885	0.141	103
avg		9180.12	0.368	113.335	35.704	1.294	0.453	0.872	0.086	96.9
std		617.5	0.025	7.623	2.080	0.047	0.018	0.012	0.017	6.4

wide" (the 162 countries in the data set) GDP valuation of \$30.6T, while an average of 30 trials in the synthetic network for that year estimated \$885.7B of trade out of a simulated \$42.0T. Subsequent years produced similar metrics well within reasonable parameters for our randomized modelling of GDP weights.

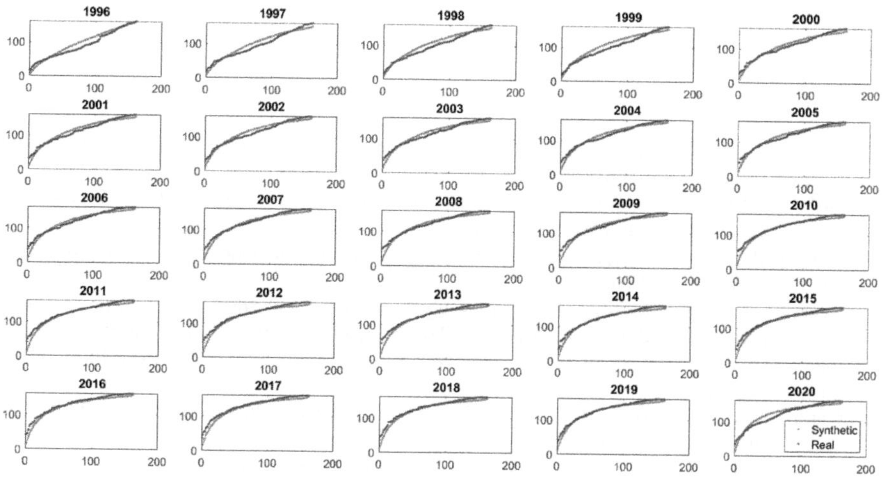

Fig. 4 Degree distribution of the real WTW (in blue) of the retained 162 countries and the synthetic WTW (in red) created from the bootstrapped 1996 GDP values

5 Conclusions and Further Directions

In this work, we presented a GDP growth-based, time-dependent world trade model to forecast future synthetic networks of the WTW. Despite the underlying complexity and geopolitical considerations likely driving real-world behavior, we find that the single macroscopic measure of GDP can adequately drive the time-evolution of the WTW. The model approximates, to a surprisingly high degree of accuracy, the real network degree distribution, clustering behavior, and other relevant topological characteristics.

Future work may find value in more appropriate GDP approximations and edge weight adjustments. While individual countries may slightly differ, global GDP growth rates appear to follow a Cauchy distribution, vice our simplified linear model [14]. This application could improve our model's ability to match real-world data years in the future, as a small error in our approximation could compound year-by-year. Additional consideration of the edge weight adjustments could likewise be fruitful: instead of heuristically tying edge weights to changes in an individual country's GDP, a distributional analysis of edge weights may improve model performance.

It is our hope that this lightweight, intuitive model can be used in the future to demonstrate, reproduce, and analyze the economic effects of major world events to yield further insights into the nature of our complex global trade system.

References

1. Albert, R., Barabási, A.: Statistical mechanics of complex networks. Rev. Mod. Phys. **74**(1), 47 (2002)
2. Caldarelli, G., Capocci, A., De Los Rios, P., Munoz, M.A.: Scale-free networks from varying vertex intrinsic fitness. Phys. Rev. Lett. **89**(25), 258702 (2002)
3. DESA/UNSD, United Nations Comtrade database. Annual goods trade: 1996–2020. Accessed 3 Feb 2022. https://comtrade.un.org/data/
4. Elliot, M.L., Goyal, S., Teytelboym, A.: Networks and economic policy. Oxf. Rev. Econ. Policy 35, 565–585 (2019). Winter
5. Frieze, A., Karoński, M.: Introduction to Random Graphs. Cambridge University Press (2016)
6. Garlaschelli D., Di Matteo, T., Aste, T., Caldarelli, G., Loffredo, M.I.: Interplay between topology and dynamics in the World Trade Web. Eur. Phys. J. B **57**(2), 159–164 (2007). arXiv: physics/0701030
7. Garlaschelli, D., Loffredo, M.I.: Patterns of link reciprocity in directed networks. Phys. Rev. Lett. **93**(26), 268701 (2004)
8. Garlaschelli, D., Loffredo, M.I.: Structure and evolution of the world trade network. Phys. Stat. Mech. Appl. **355**(1), 138–144 (2005)
9. Holme, P., Saramäki, J.: Temporal networks. Phys. Rep. **519**(3), 97–125 (2012)
10. Lagarias, J.C., Reeds, J.A., Wright, M.H., Wright, P.E.: Convergence properties of the nelder-mead simplex method in low dimensions. SIAM J. Optim. **9**(1), 112–147 (1998)
11. Mata, A.S.D.: Complex networks: a mini-review. Braz. J. Phys. 658–672 (2020)
12. Serrano, M., Boguñá, M.: Topology of the world trade web. Phys. Rev. E **68**, 015101 (2003)
13. The World Bank. Gdp (current us $)—world. Accessed 23 Feb 2022. https://databank.worldbank.org/home.aspx
14. Williams, M.A., Baek, G., Li, Y., Park, L.Y., Zhao, W.: Global evidence on the distribution of gdp growth rates. Phys. Stat. Mech. Appl. **468**, 750–758 (2017)

Co-Attention Based Multi-contextual Fake News Detection

Paritosh Kapadia, Akrati Saxena, Bhaskarjyoti Das, Yulong Pei, and Mykola Pechenizkiy

Abstract In recent years, the propagation of fake news on social media has emerged as a major challenge. Several approaches have been proposed to detect fake news on social media using the content of the microblogs and news-propagation network. In this work, we propose a method, named FND-NUP (**F**ake **N**ews **D**etection with **N**ews content, **U**ser profiles and **P**ropagation networks), to detect fake news using users' profile features, fake news content, and the propagation network. We use graph attention networks (GAT) to learn users representations using users' profile features and news propagation networks. Next, we use co-attention technique to simultaneously learn the graph attention and the news content attention vectors, that will subsequently use to detect fake news. The derived co-attention weights allow our framework to provide the propagation graph-level and news article word-level explanations, respectively. We demonstrate that FND-NUP method outperforms state-of-the-art propagation-based and content-based fake news detection approaches.

1 Introduction

The emergence of social media platforms, such as Twitter or Facebook, has transformed the way people communicate with each other as a shared content might be available to millions of people just in a few seconds. The easy sharing of the

P. Kapadia · A. Saxena (✉) · Y. Pei · M. Pechenizkiy
Eindhoven University of Technology, Eindhoven, The Netherlands
e-mail: a.saxena@tue.nl

P. Kapadia
e-mail: p.kapadia@student.tue.nl

Y. Pei
e-mail: y.pei.1@tue.nl

M. Pechenizkiy
e-mail: m.pechenizkiy@tue.nl

B. Das
PES University, Bangalore, India
e-mail: bhaskarjyotidas@pesu.pes.edu

D. Pacheco et al. (eds.), *Complex Networks XIII*, Springer Proceedings in Complexity,
https://doi.org/10.1007/978-3-031-17658-6_7

information is very helpful for spreading useful information in situations, such as disaster response, social awareness, and so on. However, on the other side, these platforms have also been exploited for sharing fake news, misinformation, personal propaganda, or biased opinion that can have severe impacts. The adverse outcomes of fake news spread, such as the manipulation during the elections or the creation of panic during a disaster, have been observed in past events [5, 9]. It has motivated researchers to design methods for fake news detection and mitigation [20].

Existing approaches of fake news detection have used three types of features. The first kind of features are content-based that use linguistic features of the news based on characters, words, sentences, and the document as a whole [19]. Commonly used linguistic features are lexical and syntactic features that include frequency of stop-words, number of exclamation and question marks, parts of speech (POS) tagging, readability of text, usage of function words, and so on [19]. Some other features specific to social networking platform are the number or proportion of external links (URLs) and hashtags (which are trending topic names prefixed with a '#') [2]. Some works also have used high level textual features, including polarity that captures the positive or negative sentiment in the text, subjectivity as fake news content might lack objectivity [15], and disagreement [19].

The second type of features for fake news detection are user-based features that include the features of the user who creates a particular post and the users who react to it further by liking, sharing, commenting, or replying [25]. These features include followers and friends count, is the user verified, user's bio, the age of user-account, the number of microblogs posted by the user, and so on [2]. The third kind of features are network-based features that consist of the social network of users engaged in spreading the news or the *propagation network* based on the spreading pattern of the news on social media [8].

In this work, we propose a framework named FND-NUP (**F**ake **N**ews **D**etection with **N**ews content, **U**ser profiles, and **P**ropagation networks) that combines the propagation based, news-content based, and user-profile based features for the fake news detection task. The proposed method first learns the vector representation for users and news content, and then the co-attention mechanism is applied to learn the relationship by combining the representations of users and news content. Finally, the model classifies a news as fake or real using the learned attention-based feature representations of news. To interpret the predictions, the derived co-attention weights allow our framework to provide the propagation graph-level and news article word-level explanations, respectively. We verify the proposed method on real-world fake news datasets and the results show that the proposed method outperforms state-of-the-art methods.

2 Related Work

News shared as a microblog on a social networking platform leads to the engagement of other users with the news by liking, commenting, or sharing the post further to their 'followers' or 'friends.' The features of the news content, the users engaged with the news, and the diffusion pattern of the news on social media are the main features used to classify the fake news and real news.

It is observed that the fake news propagates differently than the real news and diffuses at a higher speed with a wider reach [26]. Propagation-based fake news detection methods consider the social context information, such as who shared the news, how the news propagates on the network, and how the engaged users are connected with each other [6, 14, 19]. Rath et al. [18] proposed a graph attention based method, called SCARLET, to predict the fake news spreader using how the historical behavioral data and network structure of a fake news spreader differs from other users. Shu et al. [22] proposed a fake news detection method using co-attention network based on user's historical tweets and news content. However, it is a purely content-based approach and does not use news propagation information or user information, such as user profile or stance. In a recent work, Lu et al. [12] proposed a neural-network based model, called GCAN, based on the news content and retweet sequence, and then they applied co-attention mechanism to detect fake news [22]. However, the structural information of news diffusion over the network and users' posts and historical information are not considered.

Bian at el. [1] proposed a GNN-based model, called Bi-GCN (Bi-Directional Graph Convolutional Networks), that considers bidirectional rumour propagation networks to explore the characteristics of both top-down and bottom-up propagation. The proposed approach focuses only on the propagation of rumours through posts, hence the information of news article and the users spreading the rumour (user profile features) are not considered in this approach. Liu and Wu [10] modeled the news propagation as a multivariate time series, and based on that, they proposed a classifier by incorporating both Recurrent Neural Network (RNN) and Convolutional Neural Network (CNN) to detect fake news.

The propagation-based methods have made remarkable progress to detect fake news at an early stage; however, when a news is posted on a social media, we have very limited social context information. Hence, mining the news content is highly useful in early detecting the fake news. Monti et al. [14] proposed a geometric deep learning based model that uses heterogeneous features based on news content, social networks of users, and the credibility of information based on stance, and showed that the fake news can be flagged effectively at the early stage of the propagation. Dou et al. [4] proposed a GNN based model, called UPFD, that considers the news article features, users' historical posts, and propagation network based features to detect fake news. The proposed model learns the news textual embedding and graph representations of engaged users separately, and then concatenates them to train a neural classifier for identifying the fake news. In our work, we use news content, users' profile features, and their historical data to early detect the fake news, and we have compared our model with the above discussed models.

3 Problem Statement

Given a news article a posted by user u, its propagation network on a social network is denoted by $\mathcal{G}(a, u)$. In the propagation network, each user node u who was involved in spreading the news is associated with its profile feature p, and historical tweets c. For historical data, we use the latest 200 tweets (including original tweets, retweets, and replies) of a user as considered in other works [4, 16, 17]. In the fake news detection, given a news article a and its associated propagation network $\mathcal{G}$, as well as user profile p and historical tweets c, we aim to predict whether it is fake news or not. Thus, this problem is mapped into a binary classification task. Formally, given a news article a and propagation network $\mathcal{G}$, our task is to predict whether a is fake or not, i.e., $\mathcal{F} : a, \mathcal{G}, p, c \longrightarrow \{0, 1\}$ such that:

$$\mathcal{F}(a, \mathcal{G}, p, c) = \begin{cases} 1, \text{ if } a \text{ is fake news,} \\ 0, \text{ otherwise.} \end{cases}$$

4 Methodology

Our fake news detection framework FND-NUP requires three inputs, (i) news article content, (ii) its propagation network, and (iii) users' attributes (including users' profiles and recent 200 tweets), that is shown in Fig. 1. In brief, FND-NUP consists of three steps: (i) embedding learning which learns both user embedding and news embedding; (ii) co-attention which fuses user node representations and the news article encoding; and (iii) news classification which predicts the news to be fake or real.

In detail, to learn user node embedding, a GNN, e.g., Graph Convolutional Networks (GCN) [7] and Graph Attention Networks (GAT) [24], are utilized on the prop-

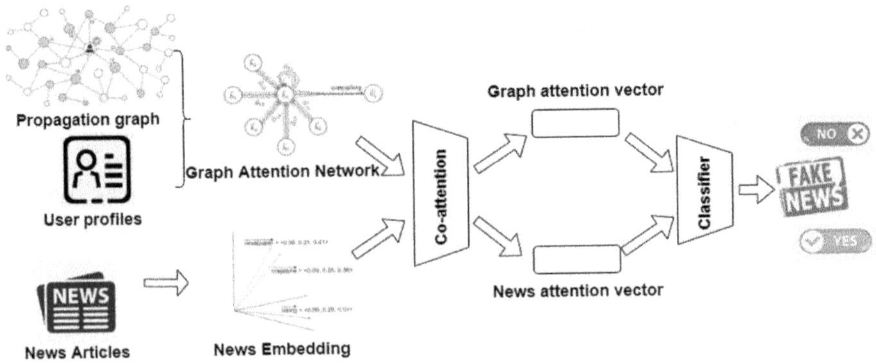

Fig. 1 Pipeline of proposed fake news detection framework

agation network based on retweet information and user attributes including users' profiles and tweets. To encode the news articles, a pre-trained word embedding is used directly. In specific we test word2vec [13] and BERT [3] as the pre-trained models in our experiments. To combine news propagation and news content, a co-attention [11] component is employed to integrate representation of news. Finally, the integrated representation will be used to classify the news. Next, we introduce the details of user node embedding and co-attention mechanism.

4.1 User Node Embedding Learning

In our work, we use a GAT to learn user node embedding using the propagation network and node attributes.

Propagation network construction The Twitter API does not provide the entire propagation network of a given tweet. To construct the news propagation networks, we follow a similar method as used in [4, 6, 14]. Consider a news article shared by a user n_0. We now consider the list of users who retweeted the news, ordered by time. This list of users is represented by $\{n_1, n_2, \ldots n_k\}$. The news propagation network is constructed in the following manner.

- In order to determine the edges between two users in the propagation network, if an account u_i retweets a news after one of the accounts it follows has shared it, the news is assumed to spread from the account that shared it the most recently to the account u_i.
- If the account u_i retweets a tweet from an account that it was not following, the news is considered to spread from the account with the highest number of followers to u_i.

User node attributes We experiment two user node attributes in this work, namely user profile features and user historical tweets. Both of these features can be used as user node attributes during the training of GNN.

- **User-profile features**: We use a 10 dimensional user-profile feature with the following attributes: whether the user is verified, whether geospatial-positioning is enabled, the number of followers, the number of friends, the number of favourite tweets, the number of lists, the creation date of the account, the number of words in the user description, and the number of words in the user screen name.
- **User-tweet features**: In order to model user-tweet features, we follow a similar approach as used in [4, 16, 17]. We use the recent 200 tweets of each user and encode them using word embedding techniques.

4.2 Co-Attention Mechanism

We employ the co-attention mechanism [11] which jointly reasons about graph attention and news article attention. Consider the news content encoding $C \in \mathbb{R}^{d \times N}$ and the latent node representation of the propagation graph $G \in \mathbb{R}^{g \times M}$, the affinity matrix $A \in \mathbb{R}^{M \times N}$ is calculated as $A = tanh(G^T \mathbf{W}_b \mathbf{C})$ where $\mathbf{W}_b \in \mathbb{R}^{d \times g}$ is the weight matrix. Affinity matrix is used as a feature to learn to news content and graph attention maps H_c and H_g as follow:

$$\begin{aligned} H_c &= \tanh(W_c C + (W_g G) A) \\ H_g &= \tanh(W_g G + (W_c C) A^T) \end{aligned} \tag{1}$$

where $W_c \in \mathbb{R}^{k \times d}$ and $W_g \in \mathbb{R}^{k \times g}$. Intuitively, the affinity matrix A serves as a transformation matrix between the graph attention space and the news content attention space.

The attention probabilities are generated by applying the softmax function:

$$\begin{aligned} a^c &= softmax(w_{hc}^T H^c) \\ a^g &= softmax(w_{hg}^T H^g) \end{aligned} \tag{2}$$

where $w_{hc}, w_{hg} \in \mathbb{R}^k$, and $a^c \in \mathbb{R}^M$ and $a^g \in \mathbb{R}^N$ are the attention probabilities for the news content and the graph user node embeddings, respectively. The affinity matrix A is responsible for transforming the graph user representation space to news content representation space, and vice a versa for A^T. Finally, the attention vectors are aggregated in the following manner:

$$\hat{c} = \sum_{n=1}^{N} a_n^c c_n, \quad \hat{g} = \sum_{t=1}^{T} a_t^g g_t \tag{3}$$

where $\hat{c} \in \mathbb{R}^d$ and $\hat{g} \in \mathbb{R}^g$ are the attention vectors for news content features and graph user features, respectively.

In order to obtain the final representations, we concatenate the feature vectors $\hat{c}$ and $\hat{g}$ to obtain the final representation, $\mathbf{r} = [\hat{c}, \hat{g}]$. This final representation is then passed into a multi-layer feed-forward neural network in order to make a final prediction of the label, i.e., whether the news is fake or real.

5 Experiments

In the experiments, we aim to answer following research questions:

- **RQ1**: How are the performances of the proposed FND-NUP compared to state-of-the-art in detecting fake news?

- **RQ2**: Can FND-NUP generate explanations that highlights why a tweet is fake with respect to the information propagation and news content?
- **RQ3**: What are the contributions of different components of the proposed framework in detecting fake news?

5.1 Experimental Setup

We use two real-world FakeNewsNet datasets [23], which contains news articles from news sites *Politifact* and *Gossipcop*. The datsets also contain the tweet ids of the users who shared the fake news and their information.

To evaluate the performance of our proposed FND-NUP, we compare it with the following state-of-the-art fake news detection approaches: (i) BiGCN [1], (ii) GCNFN [14], (iii) UPFD [4], (iv) GNNCL [6], (v) SVMW, and (vi) SVMB. SVMW and SVMB methods use an SVM classifier to classify the news using the word2vec and BERT embeddings of the news article features, respectively. To evaluate the performance from different aspects, we utilize different evaluation measures, including accuracy, F-1 (macro and micro), recall, ROC-AUC, and AP (average precision).

5.2 Overall Performance

The overall performance can be used to answer **RQ1**. We present the results of the baselines and our model on the Gossipcop dataset in Table 1 and Politifact dataset in Table 2. We notice that our model outperforms the baselines on almost all metrics. When compared to GCNFN, our model has a better performance as GCNFN only considers the graph structure features. The GCNFN model uses a graph neural network as in our model, but does not use news content features and users' historical tweets. Therefore, it performs worse as compared to our model. SVMW and SVMB use an SVM classifier to classify the word2vec and BERT embeddings of news article features, respectively. They do not use any of the auxiliary user information, such as user profile or user tweet history features, so they perform significantly worse as compared to the proposed full model.

The performance of UPFD model is the closest to our model as it also uses news content features and historical tweet based features. The UPFD model aggregates the node representation features of the social network and news content by simply concatenating their embeddings. Still, our model is more interpretable due to the attention mechanism which provides attention vectors, and certain aspects of the features have higher attention scores as compared to others. When the distribution of these attention scores of the words in the news article and the edges in the propagation graphs are analyzed, they provide reasons about the model's prediction.

Table 1 Results on the Gossipcop dataset

Model	Accuracy	Macro-F1	Micro-F1	Recall	ROC-AUC	AP
BiGCN	0.896	0.896	0.896	0.837	0.964	0.966
GCNFN	0.891	0.891	0.891	0.870	0.950	0.955
UPFD	0.952	0.952	0.952	0.930	**0.989**	**0.990**
GNNCL	0.950	0.949	0.950	0.949	0.979	0.974
SVMW	0.668	0.667	0.668	0.611	0.727	0.745
SVMB	0.679	0.678	0.679	0.615	0.735	0.746
FND-NUP	**0.965**	**0.963**	**0.965**	**0.968**	0.982	0.983

Table 2 Results on the Politifact dataset

Model	Accuracy	Macro-F1	Micro-F1	Recall	ROC-AUC	AP
BiGCN	0.769	0.765	0.769	0.786	0.827	0.820
GCNFN	0.765	0.763	0.765	0.769	0.833	0.786
UPFD	0.805	0.803	0.805	0.849	0.892	0.909
GNNCL	0.665	0.658	0.665	0.528	0.768	0.773
SVMW	0.809	0.806	0.809	0.902	0.805	0.773
SVMB	0.564	0.562	0.564	0.515	0.629	0.611
FND-NUP	**0.869**	**0.865**	**0.869**	**0.866**	**0.952**	**0.952**

5.3 *Explainability*

To answer **RQ2** about the explainability, we refer to attention weights as they provide insights about the explainability of the results of a model [21]. We attempt to explain our results by using the attention weights of the graph attention network and the news article co-attention vectors.

Network-level explainability The distribution of the attention edge weights of GAT are used to explain the results. We compare the distribution and values of the attention scores of propagation networks corresponding to real news and fake news to explain the results of our model. User profile features can be interpreted as credibility features and the user historical tweet based features can be interpreted as stance or preference features.

A few examples of attention matrices representing real news and fake news propagation networks are displayed in Figs. 2 and 3, respectively. Fake news attention-matrix-edges generally have lower edge credibility scores as compared to real news attention matrices. The average attention score for the real news networks is 0.0244 as compared to fake news networks, whose average attention score is 0.0125.

Some fake news propagation networks are observed to form smaller clusters with reduced connectivity to the root node, as shown in Fig. 3b. This provides more scope to form echo chambers, and the news becomes more manipulated. Figure 3c presents

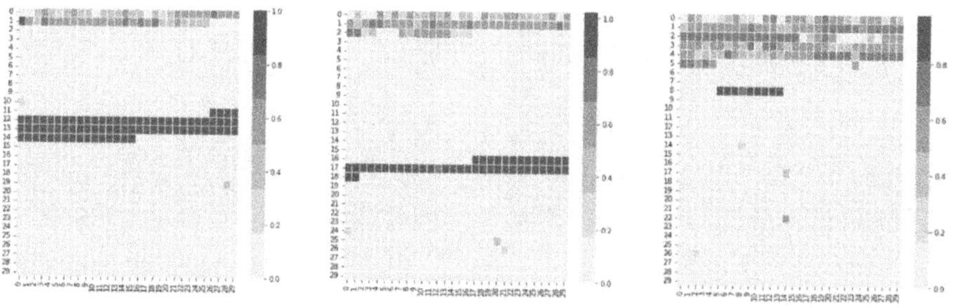

(a) Real news network with average attention score of 0.119

(b) Real news network with average attention score of 0.080

(c) Real news network with average attention score of 0.1018

Fig. 2 Examples of various real news propagation networks along with their average attention scores

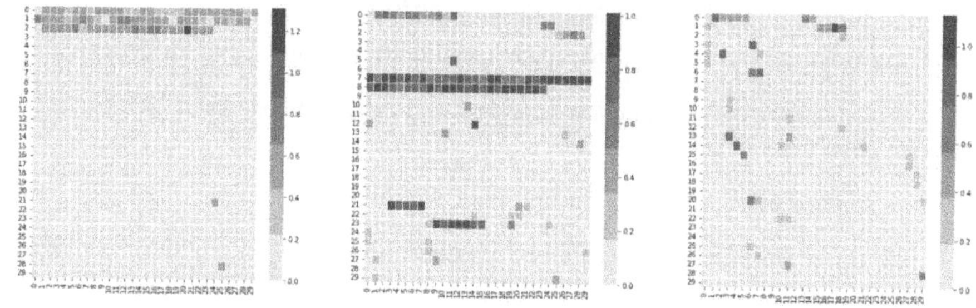

(a) Fake news network with average attention score of 0.048

(b) Fake news network with average attention score of 0.024

(c) Fake news network with average attention score of 0.083

Fig. 3 Examples of various fake news networks along with their average attention scores

a case where the root and initial edges have low credibility scores, whereas, down the propagation tree, the edges have higher credibility scores. Thus at the beginning of the news propagation, the news gets spread further due to less credible users spreading it. By comparing the examples from real news and fake news propagation networks in Figs. 2 and 3, it can be observed that (i) real news propagation generally has larger attention scores which indicate that during the spreading of real news, users have more influence on each other, and (ii) users who spread real news have stronger correlations based on users' features while users who spread fake news are not highly correlated.

Word-level explainability For word-level explainability, we study how words in an article contribute towards the news being predicted as real or fake. In the news content attention vector each word is associated with an attention score, and the magnitude of the attention score denotes its relative importance to other words that contribute to the classification of the news.

(a) Words from a fake news article

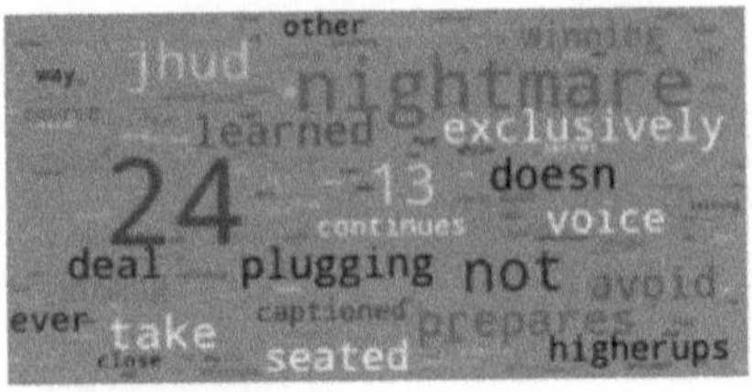

(b) Words from a fake news article

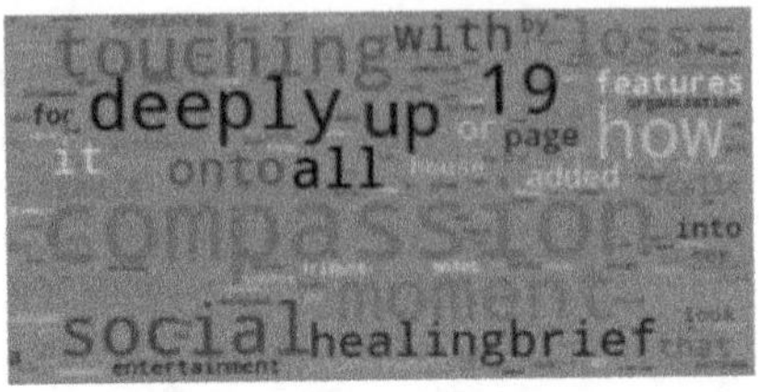

(c) Words from a real news article

Fig. 4 Visualisation of the words from news articles in Gossipcop. Words with higher importance scores are associated with larger word size

In Fig. 4, we present two examples of words from fake news articles, highlighted according to their importance scores. In Fig. 4a we see sensationalizing and attention grabbing words like 'exclusively' and 'white' with high importance scores. In Fig. 4b we see words that are not normally associated with professional genuine reporting, such as 'nightmare', and sensationalizing words like 'exclusively' also carry high importance scores. This leads to a higher likelihood of these words contributing to the final label prediction by the model. In Fig. 4c, we present an example of words from a real news article. The words are highlighted according to their importance scores. We notice that words that are sensational or cause alarm are not present in the real news article.

5.4 Ablation Analysis

The ablation analysis is conducted to answer **RQ3**. We perform ablation studies in order to validate the contribution of each component of the model for fake news detection. Particularly, we compare the following model variants:

- *Graph attention alone*
- *Using co-attention with user profile features*
- *Using co-attention with users' historical tweet features*
- *Full model: using co-attention with user tweet + user profile features*

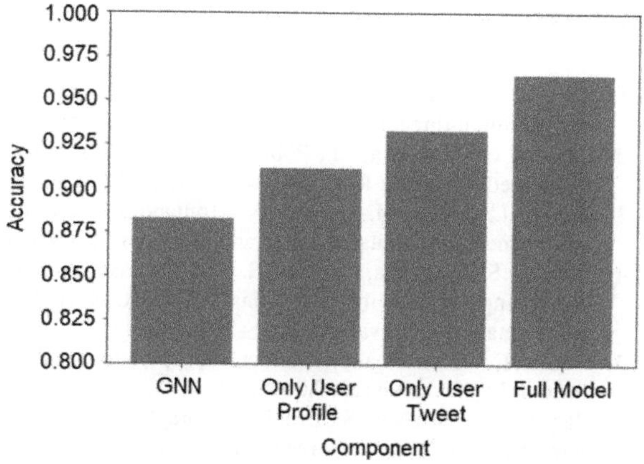

Fig. 5 Ablation analysis of the test accuracy of our model on Gossipcop

Figure 5 shows the results of ablation analysis on the Gossipcop dataset. We notice that the full model, that is, where co-attention is applied on the user node embeddings and the news article embeddings by using both the user tweet history + user profile features as the node attributes has the highest performance. We notice that the accuracy of the model is the lowest with the classification done on user node representations obtained by the graph neural network (GNN). The possible reasons are that the model ignores user profile and news article content which lead to significant information loss for news classification. The similar results were observed for the Politifact dataset.

6 Conclusion

In this work, we propose a fake news detection method, called FND-NUP, based on news content, users' profile attributes, and news propagation networks. The proposed method jointly learn the attention vectors using a co-attention mechanism on the propagation graph and news article features. We compare our method with state-of-the-art fake news detection method and the results demonstrate that our model outperforms recently proposed fake news detection models. In future, we would like to explore to integrate more advanced GNN and NLP models to improve the performance. We will further investigate the explainability of fake news detection method beyond attention mechanism.

References

1. Bian, T., Xiao, X., Xu, T., Zhao, P., Huang, W., Rong, Y., Huang, J.: Rumor detection on social media with bi-directional graph convolutional networks (2020)
2. Castillo, C., Mendoza, M., Poblete, B.: Predicting information credibility in time-sensitive social media. Internet Res. **23**(5), 560–588 (2013)
3. Devlin, J., Chang, M.-W., Lee, K., Toutanova, K.: Bert: pre-training of deep bidirectional transformers for language understanding (2018). arxiv:1810.04805
4. Dou, Y., Shu, K., Xia, C., Yu, P.S., Sun, L.: User preference-aware fake news detection. In: Proceedings of the 44th International ACM SIGIR Conference on Research and Development in Information Retrieval, pp. 2051–2055 (2021)
5. Ferrara, E.: Disinformation and social bot operations in the run up to the 2017 french presidential election (2017). arXiv:1707.00086
6. Han, Y., Karunasekera, S., Leckie, C.: Graph neural networks with continual learning for fake news detection from social media (2020). arXiv:2007.03316
7. Kipf, T.N., Welling, M.: Semi-supervised classification with graph convolutional networks (2016). arXiv:1609.02907
8. Kwon, S., Cha, M., Jung, K., Chen, W., Wang, Y.: Prominent features of rumor propagation in online social media. In *2013 IEEE 13th International Conference on Data Mining*, pp. 1103–1108. IEEE (2013)
9. Lazer David, M.J., Baum, M.A., Benkler, Y., Berinsky, A.J., Greenhill, K.M., Menczer, F., Metzger, M.J., Nyhan, B., Pennycook, G., Rothschild, D. et al.: The science of fake news. Science **359**(6380), 1094–1096 (2018)
10. Liu, Y., Brook Wu, Y.-F.: Early detection of fake news on social media through propagation path classification with recurrent and convolutional networks. In Thirty-Second AAAI Conference on Artificial Intelligence (2018)
11. Jiasen, L., Yang, J., Batra, D., Parikh, D.: Hierarchical question-image co-attention for visual question answering. Adv. Neural Inf. Process. Syst. **29**, 289–297 (2016)
12. Lu, Y.-J., Li, C.-T.: Gcan: Graph-aware co-attention networks for explainable fake news detection on social media. In: Proceedings of the 58th Annual Meeting of the Association for Computational Linguistics, pp. 505–514 (2020)
13. Mikolov, T., Chen, K., Corrado, G., Dean, J.: Efficient estimation of word representations in vector space (2013). arXiv:1301.3781
14. Monti, F., Frasca, F., Eynard, D., Mannion, D., Bronstein, M.M.: Fake news detection on social media using geometric deep learning (2019). arXiv:1902.06673
15. Potthast, M., Kiesel, J., Reinartz, K., Bevendorff, J., Stein, B.: A stylometric inquiry into hyperpartisan and fake news. In: Proceedings of the 56th Annual Meeting of the Association for Computational Linguistics, vol. 1: Long Papers, pp. 231–240 (2018) <error l="305" c="Invalid command: paragraph not started." />
16. Qian, J., ElSherief, M., Belding, E.M., Wang, W.Y.: Leveraging intra-user and inter-user representation learning for automated hate speech detection. In: Proceedings of NAACL-HLT, pp. 118–123 (2018)
17. Rangel, F., Giachanou, A., Ghanem, B.H.H., Rosso, P.: Overview of the 8th author profiling task at pan 2020: profiling fake news spreaders on twitter. In: CEUR Workshop Proceedings, vol. 2696, pp. 1–18. Sun SITE Central Europe (2020)
18. Rath, B., Morales, X., Srivastava, J.: Scarlet: explainable attention based graph neural network for fake news spreader prediction. In: Pacific-Asia Conference on Knowledge Discovery and Data Mining, pp. 714–727. Springer, Berlin (2021)
19. Saxena, A., Saxena, P., Reddy, H.: Fake news detection techniques for social media. In: Principles of Social Networking, pp. 325–354. Springer, Berlin (2022)
20. Saxena, A., Saxena, P., Reddy, H:. Fake news propagation and mitigation techniques: a survey. In: Principles of Social Networking, pp. 355–386. Springer, Berlin (2022)

21. Serrano, S., Smith, N.A.: Is attention interpretable? In: Proceedings of the 57th Annual Meeting of the Association for Computational Linguistics, pp. 2931–2951. Association for Computational Linguistics, Florence, Italy (2019)
22. Shu, K., Cui, L., Wang, S., Lee, D., Liu, H.: defend: Explainable fake news detection. In: Proceedings of the 25th ACM SIGKDD International Conference on Knowledge Discovery and Data Mining, pp. 395–405 (2019)
23. Shu, K., Mahudeswaran, D., Wang, S., Lee, D., Liu, H.: Fakenewsnet: a data repository with news content, social context, and spatiotemporal information for studying fake news on social media. Big Data **8**(3), 171–188 (2020)
24. Velickovic, P., Cucurull, G., Casanova, A., Romero, A., Lio, P., Bengio, Y.: Graph attention networks. stat **1050**, 20 (2017)
25. Vosoughi, S., Mohsenvand, M.N., Roy, D.: Rumor gauge: predicting the veracity of rumors on twitter. ACM Trans. Knowl. Discov. Data (TKDD) **11**(4), 50 (2017)
26. Vosoughi, S., Roy, D., Aral, S.: The spread of true and false news online. Science **359**(6380), 1146–1151 (2018)

Correlation Financial Networks of an Unstable Stock Market: Empirical Study

Sergei Sidorov, Alexey Faizliev, Vladimir Balash, Dmitriy Melnichuk, and Alexey Grigoriev

Abstract Correlation networks are a popular way to display financial information due to their simplicity and ease of interpretation. However, the assets returns for two companies that share a common cause may be spuriously correlated. To avoid this, it is suggested to use a partial correlation. This paper is devoted to the analysis of the dynamics of the Pearson correlation network and the partial correlation network based on the Russian stock market asset returns and their comparison. The Russian financial market was chosen as the object of study in our work for the following reason: from 2012 to 2022, the Russian economic system was affected by numerous negative factors and shocks (while during this period the economies of most other countries showed stable growth after the 2008 crisis). The main research question of this paper is as follows: do the behavior patterns of market networks for fairly stable financial systems differ from the behavior patterns of networks for volatile systems that are experiencing multiple shocks?

1 Introduction

Representation of complex systems in the form of network is a convenient method of their analysis. This is due to the network's ability to express relationships between components with a simple model that is applicable in various fields.

One of the common ways to build a financial network is to use Pearson correlation coefficient between stock returns to construct the corresponding minimum spanning tree from the resulting weighted graph. Typically, such papers confirm that companies are grouped in MST in accordance with sectors of economy they belong to [9]. Paper [13] further examines the impact of a market crisis on the minimum spanning tree structure. The authors say that the length of the tree decreases during the crisis

This work was supported by the Ministry of Science and Higher Education of the Russian Federation in the framework of the basic part of the scientific research state task, project FSRR-2020-0006.

S. Sidorov (✉) · A. Faizliev · V. Balash · D. Melnichuk · A. Grigoriev
Saratov State University, Saratov 410012, Russia
e-mail: sidorovsp@info.sgu.ru

D. Pacheco et al. (eds.), *Complex Networks XIII*, Springer Proceedings in Complexity,
https://doi.org/10.1007/978-3-031-17658-6_8

(i.e., asset returns become more correlated). Paper [4] creates networks from the correlation matrix and examine what happens to the network structure when a threshold is set. Correlation coefficients with an absolute value below a certain threshold are set equal to zero, while coefficients above the threshold are equal to one.

The paper [14] shows that many links in the correlation network are noise. However, an asset with a higher eigenvector centrality usually contains information that affects all stocks (for example, an increase in interest rates). The authors also analyse the next-largest eigenvectors, and find that they tend to have higher values for related stocks, for example, those in the same sector or doing business in similar regions. Finally, they show that the largest eigenvector is quite stable over time.

Correlation coefficient gives a simple interpretable model, but it has a drawback. Two companies can be correlated due to a common cause (another company), which can result in the false link between them. The use of partial correlations eliminates the influence of the third variable [7, 11]. The authors of these works show that partial correlation networks have much less volatile intensity than correlation networks, but they are less stable. It is also noted that in the US stock markets, the financial sector is central and it retains its positions throughout the entire period under review.

Another example of using partial correlation is presented in [17], which compares minimal spanning trees constructed using both Pearson and partial correlation coefficients for various stock indices. The partial correlation matrix was calculated as the inverse correlation matrix. They found that the structure of centrality in a minimum spanning tree based on partial correlation is more informative than the structure based on Pearson correlation.

It should be noted that the previous study [11] focused on the relatively stable US financial market. However, of scientific interest is also the study of the comparative behavior of Pearson networks and partial correlation networks for financial markets, which were extremely volatile and experienced many different shocks during the analyzed period. The Russian financial market was chosen as the object of study in our work for the following reason: from 2012 to 2022, the Russian economic system was affected by numerous negative factors and shocks (while during this period the economies of most other countries showed stable growth after the 2008 crisis), including the fall in oil prices in the second half of 2014, pressure caused by sanctions imposed on Russia after the annexation of Crimea to Russia, structural problems of Russian economy and low GDP growth compared to other countries, another drop in oil prices in 2018, a crisis caused by the pandemic in 2020–2022 years, a sharp drop in oil prices at the beginning of 2020, financial and economic uncertainty caused by the political crisis in connection with the deployment of Russian troops near the borders with Ukraine in the summer of 2021 and in January–February 2022. All of the above factors and the shocks had caused a negative impact on the stability of the Russian stock market, making it rather volatile and unpredictable. These characteristics make it interesting for our analysis, allowing us to see how both Pearson and partial correlation networks behave for unstable financial systems.

In this regard, the main research question of this paper is as follows: do the behavior patterns of market networks obtained in the work [11] for fairly stable financial systems differ from the behavior patterns of networks for volatile systems that are experiencing multiple shocks?

Thus, unlike the paper [11], which examines the US stock market in the period from 01/03/2000 to 12/05/2017, in our study we construct both the Pearson correlation and the partial correlation networks from daily log returns of 99 Russian companies from 01/01/2012 to 23/02/2022 using the Ledoit-Wolf covariance method. This allows us to obtain an invertible covariance matrix, which is required to estimate the partial correlation matrix. We construct networks for 75 consecutive overlapping 300-day periods using sliding window procedure. The purpose of the study is to compare the dynamics of the structural properties of these networks.

The paper is organized as follows. Section 2 presents definitions and notations used in the article and empirical results, including the data and methodology used to construct networks. In Sect. 3 constructed networks are considered in the context of the economy sectors and community structure. Conclusions are presented in Sect. 5.

2 Correlation Networks

2.1 Definitions, Notations

An extensive bulk of literature is devoted to the study of the connectivity between elements of economic systems using measures based on correlation coefficients. A common way to measure the relationship between financial assets returns is to calculate a matrix of correlation coefficients for a given period. The values of the sample correlation coefficients can vary significantly over time, for example, they can vary greatly during tranquil and crisis sub-periods. Simple factor models (see e.g. [2]) assume that the observed returns are added under the influence of one or several factors common to all assets. If in some sub-period the variance of the common factor increases, then this also causes an increase in the values of sample correlations. This phenomenon can be interpreted depending on how shocks are propagated as contagion or herding [5]. When considering rolling correlation, it is interesting to know the effect on the magnitude of correlations between returns or volatilities of individual shocks. An approach to the study of the impact of hotel shocks on the frequency of connectivity is developed in [1, 6].

In order for correlation matrix (C) to be calculated for stocks, it is required to use time series of prices (Adj Close) $r_i(t)$ for each company i at the same time period t. Next, to smooth the oscillations we use log returns $Y_i(t)$ of a company i in a time period $[t - \Delta t, t]$ defined by $Y_i(t) = \ln r_i(t) - \ln r_i(t - \Delta t)$, where $\Delta t = 1$ for daily prices.

Pearson correlation matrix (C) is calculated for each pair of companies i and j as follows

$$C_{ij} = \frac{\Sigma_{ij}}{\sqrt{\Sigma_{ii}\Sigma_{jj}}}, \tag{1}$$

where Σ is covariance matrix.

The partial correlation matrix (P) is calculated by

$$P_{ij} = -\frac{\Theta_{ij}}{\sqrt{\Theta_{ii}\Theta_{jj}}}, \tag{2}$$

where Θ is inverse of the covariance matrix or the precision matrix. It should be noted that the sample size is not large enough for consistency estimation of covariance matrix. Therefore, the inverse covariance matrix does not always exist. To solve this problem, we use the Ledoit-Wolf covariance method [8]. This method is aimed to give a positive definite invertible matrix. The Ledoit-Wolf covariance is based on shrinkage where we combine the sample covariance matrix S (which may have high variance but small bias) with the known matrix with some desirable properties (i.e. it has low variance but large bias). A linear combination of two matrices is composed by $\Sigma_{\text{lw}} = (1-\rho)S + \rho\text{tr}(S)I$, where $tr(S)$ is the trace of matrix S, and I is the identity matrix.

2.2 *Data and Methodology*

As initial data, we take the daily adjusted closing prices of 99 Russian companies from 10 sectors (Technology and Communication companies are merged into one sector) (Table 1). The trading period on the Moscow stock exchange was taken from 01/01/2012 to 23/02/2022. Thus, there are only 2540 traded days. Missing trading days were filled with values of previous days traded, or if data is missing from the beginning, from the first day the stock is traded. In total, such days do not exceed 15% of the total number.

Since financial time series in our dataset is non-stationary, we apply the 300-days-long window and slide along it for 30 days each time to obtain a sample where we can assume the data is stationary, giving us 75 windows overall. The returns for each window are normalized using the Z-score to obtain zero mean and unit standard deviation. While correlations are normalized by definition, this procedure is carried out to assist the shrinkage procedure, since the normalization reduces the amount of shrinkage required which allows us to capture more relationships.

For our study we use daily data from the Moscow Exchange Index (IMOEX.ME). Moscow Exchange Index is a market capitalization weighted index of the Russian stock market, which includes the most liquid securities.

Based on this dataset we construct a network for every window with use of the Ledoit-Wolf shrinkage method to find a covariance matrix and then we invert it to calculate a precision matrix. We then scale both of these matrices appropriately using (1) and (2) to find the correlation and partial correlation matrices and use these as adjacency matrices of the constructed networks. We then examine the properties of both networks and how they evolve over time.

This study uses Python 3, pandas library [10] for data manipulation and yfinance library for downloading historical trading ticker data, NumPy and SciPy [12] for gen-

Table 1 List of companies by sector

Sector	Count
Utilities (Rosseti, Mosenergo, ...)	24
Basic Materials (Norilsk Nickel, Severstal, ...)	21
Energy (Rosneft, Gazprom, Novatek ...)	14
Industrials (Aeroflot, Kamaz, ...)	11
Financial Services (Rosbank, Sberbank, ...)	8
Technology + Communication Services (Yandex, RBC, ...)	7
Consumer Defensive (Abrau-Durso, Magnit, ...)	5
Real Estate (PIK Group, HALS-Development, ...)	4
Consumer Cyclical (M.video, ...)	3
Healthcare (36.6, Human Stem Cells Institute, ...)	2

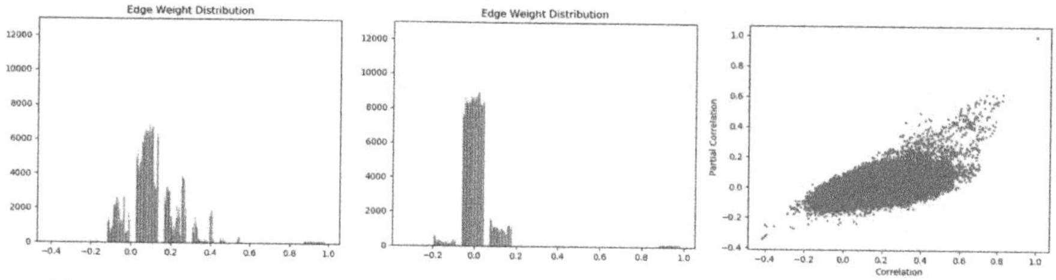

(a) Pearson correlation (b) Partial correlation (c) Scatter plot

Fig. 1 Distributions of correlation coefficients and scatter plot of the correlation coefficient for an edge against that of the partial correlation coefficient

eral scripting, sklearn for the implementation of the Ledoit Wolf estimation methods, statsmodels for some of the statistical analysis, matplotlib for plotting, Networkx for the network analysis.

2.3 *Empirical Results*

Firstly, let us compare the distribution of Pearson's correlation coefficients (C), obtained by the formula (1), with the distribution of partial correlation coefficients (P) defined in (2). Their histograms and the scatter plot linking the two quantities are shown in Fig. 1. As can be seen from these plots, the values of P are less than the corresponding values of C, and also more often have negative values. Thus, P reduces the strength of indirect correlations, i.e. correlations caused by the influence of a common factor.

Secondly, we display the networks inferred from the first window. Since the graphs are complete, we display the edges whose weights correspond to the 300 largest

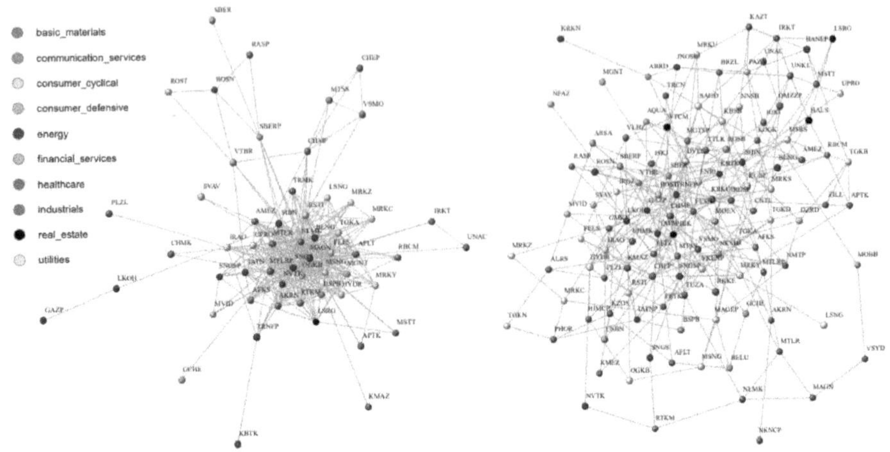

(a) Pearson correlation (b) Partial correlation

Fig. 2 Pearson correlation and Partial correlation networks for the first window

absolute values. The C network has isolated nodes, so we only display the largest connected component (56 companies out of 99 remained) (Fig. 2). At the same time the P network remains connected (there are 98 companies left) (Fig. 2). Note that both networks are characterized by sector-specific clustering, which is especially pronounced for the C network. It is also worth noting that the P network has a more uniform degree distribution, while the network C is more likely to be characterized by a power-law degree distribution.

One of the main research questions of the paper is to compare the stability of networks built on the basis of correlations C and P (using the values of the correlations as the weights of the edges connecting the corresponding assets). For this purpose, we study how one of the network centrality measures, namely the eigenvector centrality, changes over time. First, we look at how the largest eigenvalue changes over time for both networks. The calculation results are shown in Fig. 3a, b. It can be seen that the largest eigenvalues for the matrices based on partial correlations P are much less than the largest eigenvalues for the matrices constructed with the use of the Pearson correlations C. Moreover, they vary relatively little compared to the largest eigenvalues of the C-matrices. Perhaps this indicates the removal of market mode when using P. Also noticeable is a strong decrease in the eigenvalues during the 2020 pandemic and then a sharp increase. Perhaps this is due to the rapid recovery of financial markets.

As another indicator of the stability of a network, we will look at how its central vertices change over time. For this purpose, we normalize the eigenvectors so that their sum is 1, and then we calculate the difference between them for adjacent windows using the L_2 norm. As it can be seen from Fig. 3, for the network built using the P matrix, there are larger changes in the values of the largest eigenvectors

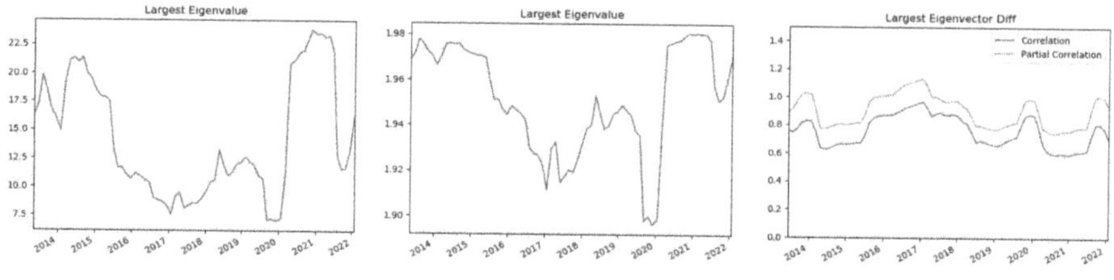

(a) C-network (b) P-network (c) Leading eigenvectors

Fig. 3 Largest eigenvalue in the networks and change in the normalized leading eigenvectors

than for the Pearson correlation network. Perhaps, this plot reflects some Russian macroeconomic changes. It can be noted that the difference between eigenvectors from adjacent windows decreases during periods of financial crisis.

3 Network Communities

3.1 Sector Centrality

Next, we consider both the partial correlation and the Pearson correlation financial networks in the context of the economy sectors. To quantify the impact of each sector in the networks we will use two measures: degree centrality and eigenvector centrality. Recall that degree centrality is defined as the number of links of a given node. The eigenvector centrality corresponds to the largest eigenvalue, with its components normalized so that their sum equals 1. The largest eigenvector reflects the market mode and the impact of the entire market on a particular company.

Note that we assume the existence of negative links in the networks, and therefore, some nodes may have negative centrality, which is difficult to interpret. By this reason, we normalize them in such a way that the sum of the centrality of all nodes would be equal to 1. As an indicator of the centrality of a sector, we take the average centrality for all companies in a given sector of the economy. Figure 4 show the degree centralities for all sectors in both networks. The plots show that the sector centrality indicators for the partial correlation network have a much smaller spread than for the networks built on the basis of the Pearson correlation. The financial and energy sectors have the highest average centrality over most of the time frame under consideration. Interestingly, during the 2020 pandemic, the average centrality of the health sector declined quite dramatically. This is due to a decrease in correlation with other sectors.

Figure 5 show the average eigenvector centrality for the sectors in each network (calculated for thresholded version of networks). The plots show that the results are very close. We note that the financial and energy sectors dominate in the sense of centrality over the period. Of particular interest is the fact that the sector centrality

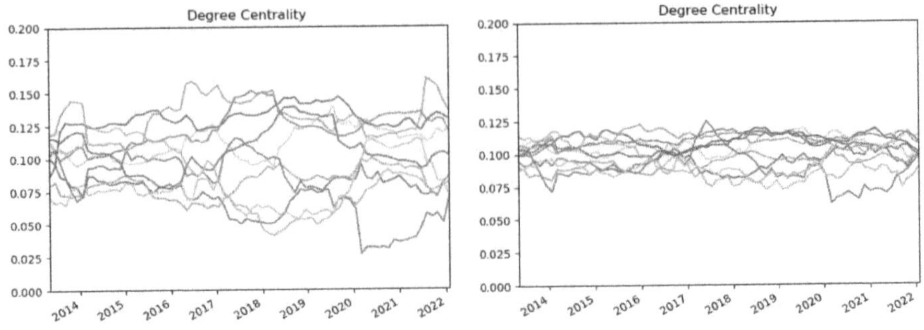

(a) Pearson correlation (b) Partial correlation

Fig. 4 Mean degree centrality for each sector over time for **a** correlation network, for **b** partial correlation network

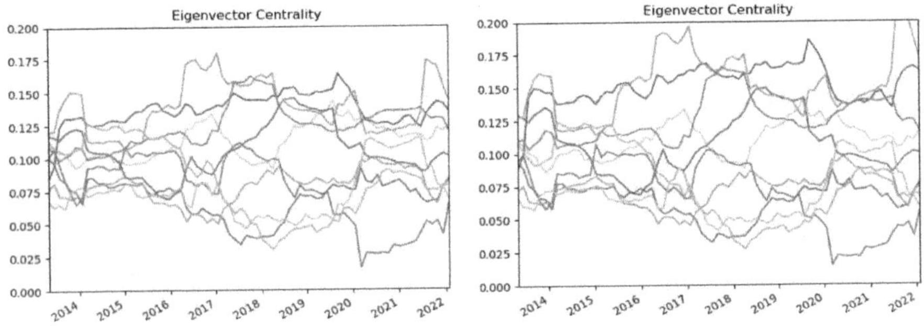

(a) Pearson correlation (b) Partial correlation

Fig. 5 Mean eigenvector centrality for each sector over time for **a** correlation network, for **b** partial correlation network

measures tend to get closer in times of crisis. This means that the market is more correlated during financial crises. During these periods, unrelated assets tend to be more interrelated.

3.2 Community Structure

It is clearly seen that some kind of community structure is present in financial networks. In this regard, it is of interest how well these communities fit into the sector structure. For community discovery, Louvain's algorithm was used to maximize network modularity [3]. We divide the network into positive and negative edges, and then we compute the total modularity as the scaled version of modularity for positive and negative parts of graph [11]. To assess clustering, we use the Adjusted Rand

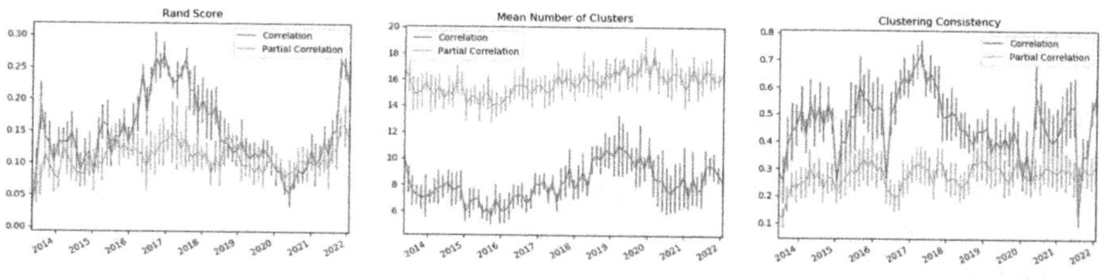

(a) ARI score (b) Number of clusters (c) Clustering Consistency

Fig. 6 Community structure over time

Index (ARI) which corrects the randomness using expected similarity for clustering within a random model, $ARI = \frac{R-E[R]}{\max(R)-E[R]}$, where R is the Rand Index [16].

Figure 6 shows the dynamics of the ARI index over time. It demonstrates how networks reflect the known sector structure. The partial correlation networks are less successful in detecting sector structure and show large variations over the time period under consideration. We assume that this is due to a decrease in indirect correlations, which leads to a decrease in success in restoring the structure of sectors. We also note that during periods of financial crises (2014 and 2020), the ARI indicator decreases for both networks. This may be due to an increase in the degree of correlation and volatility causing companies to behave more alike, which reduces the algorithm's ability to separate them [15].

Next, let us analyze how the number of clusters has changed over time (the results are in Fig. 6). As it can be seen, the Pearson correlation networks have fewer clusters than P-networks (on average 8, while P-networks have on average 17). At the same time, the number of clusters in P-network is more stable over time. The growing correlation is especially strong during a pandemic, which may cause companies to become more alike. There are 10 economic sectors in our dataset, so the method based on C-correlation is quite close in terms of the number of clusters to the true value.

Finally, consider how stable the clusters are over time. We use the Adjusted Rand Index to compare the clustering consistency between clusters from the previous and next windows (see Fig. 6). As you can see, the P-networks have a much more stable structure than the C-networks (i.e., the ARI indicator between each neighboring windows is higher, and therefore more companies are in the same cluster). For correlation networks, there were larger gaps in 2014 and 2020 with a significant decrease in consistency.

4 Comparison with S&P500 Network

On the other hand, the Pearson correlation coefficient distributions differ significantly between the IMOEX network and the $S\&P500$ network. It can be argued that the Russian stock market is less interconnected, and there are quite a lot of inverse relationships between the shares of Russian companies. In fact, this feature of the Russian stock market may be considered as a positive characteristic from the point of view of building a diversified investment portfolio. As for the community structure of the IMOEX correlation network, in contrast to the $S\&P500$ network, it is rather weakly grouped in accordance with sectors of the economy. The results showed that the Utilities, Basic Materials and Energy sectors form one large central cluster (community).

Secondly, we note that for each window the largest eigenvalue of the partial correlation matrix (as well as for the $S\&P500$ network) is much smaller and changes relatively little over time, compared to the largest eigenvalue of the Pearson correlation matrix. But unlike the $S\ \&P500$ network, the change in the largest eigenvalue for various correlation matrices over time is visually very similar and captures all the economic and political crises of the considered time horizon well. Thus, it can be argued that the partial correlations between assets for the Russian stock market did not introduce new information in the study of the change in the largest eigenvalue, i.e. unlike the $S\ \&\ P500$ network, market mode has not been completely removed. As for the difference between the eigenvectors of neighboring windows, they, as well as for the $S\ \&\ P500$ network, quite well reflect macroeconomic changes, decreasing during periods of instability in the economy associated with the political crisis in Ukraine in 2014, a new wave of sanctions in April 2018, the COVID19 pandemic (March 2020). We also note that even before the start of the military operation in Ukraine (February 24, 2022), the measure of the difference between eigenvectors had already begun to decrease.

Third, the partial correlation networks for both stock markets have a much smaller spread of sector centrality over time than the correlation networks. Sectors with few firms for both markets have much greater centrality variance. Also, as for the $S\ \&\ P500$ network, during the crises, the centralities of most sectors jump together. This indicates the strengthening of interrelations between companies due to the corresponding macroeconomic effects. The average eigenvector centrality for each sector over time has much greater variance than the degree centralities, especially for networks with partial correlation. At the same time, the financial sector is the most important for most of the time periods. This result is also consistent with the US stock markets. But unlike the $S\&P500$, the energy sector becomes the most important during crises. This is quite natural, since the oil and gas industry is still the leading sector of the Russian economy. Macroeconomic effects are especially noticeable after the political crisis between 2014 and 2015, and also during the pandemic, when all sectors move together.

Fourth, the partial correlation networks are generally less successful in detecting sector structure, although both networks show large variations over time. In times of crisis, the ARI for IMOEX networks, in contrast to its values for the US stock market, decreases for both correlation networks and partial correlation networks. This may be due to the fact that the increase in the values of correlations between assets for the Russian stock market is not so significant during crises. Correlation networks have fewer clusters than partial correlation networks. Correlation networks have a much more stable structure than partial correlation networks (there are more companies in the same cluster), although the variation for the number of sectors is noticeably higher. For both networks, one can see an increase in clustering during the crisis. This is consistent with the results for $S\ \&\ P500$. Unlike for the US stock market, the correlation network correctly predicted the number of actual sectors of the Russian economy.

5 Conclusion

In this paper we have studied the market network dynamics over time using Pearson correlation and partial correlation. Partial correlation networks for the American stock market are studied in paper [11]. Our work is aimed at reproducing the methodology of the paper, applied to the Russian stock market. It was found that:

- The partial correlation networks have more negative link weights than the correlation networks, and their weights are lower. However, there is a clear relationship between them: some edges with a higher Pearson correlation also have a higher partial correlation. This is expected since partial correlation is designed to reduce the effect of indirect correlations.
- The largest eigenvalue of the Pearson correlation network varies significantly depending on market situation, while the largest eigenvalue of the partial correlation network remains relatively constant. However, using the difference in the largest eigenvector to measure stability of the network it was found that the partial correlation networks are less stable than the Pearson correlation networks.
- In the partial correlation networks, all sectors of the economy have a fairly constant average degree centrality, which does not depend on macroeconomic factors. This finding does not apply to the correlation networks, where there is a clear difference in centrality, especially during the crisis of 2014 as well as during the 2020 pandemic.
- Using the Louvain community detection algorithm, we have tested whether sectors of the economy are replicated as clusters in networks built on the real data. It was found that partial correlation networks are less successful than correlation networks in detecting such clusters. The correlation networks also provide more stable clustering with fewer clusters than the partial correlation networks.

References

1. Baruník, J., Křehlík, T.: Measuring the frequency dynamics of financial connectedness and systemic risk. J. Financ. Econ. **16**(2), 271–296 (2018). https://doi.org/10.1093/jjfinec/nby001
2. Bekaert, G., Hodrick, R.J., Zhang, X.: International stock return comovements. J. Financ. **64**(6), 2591–2626 (2009). https://doi.org/10.1111/j.1540-6261.2009.01512.x

3. Blondel, V.D., Guillaume, J.L., Lambiotte, R., Lefebvre, E.: Fast unfolding of communities in large networks. J. Stat. Mech. Theory Exp. **2008**(10), P10008 (2008). https://doi.org/10.1088/1742-5468/2008/10/p10008
4. Boginski, V., Butenko, S., Pardalos, P.M.: Statistical analysis of financial networks. Comput. Stat. Data Anal. **48**(2), 431–443 (2005). https://doi.org/10.1016/j.csda.2004.02.004
5. Chiang, T.C., Jeon, B.N., Li, H.: Dynamic correlation analysis of financial contagion: evidence from asian markets. J. Int. Money Financ. **26**(7), 1206–1228 (2007). https://doi.org/10.1016/j.jimonfin.2007.06.005
6. Diebold, F.X., Yilmaz, K.: On the network topology of variance decompositions: measuring the connectedness of financial firms. J. Econ. **182**(1), 119–134 (2014). https://doi.org/10.1016/j.jeconom.2014.04.012
7. Kenett, D.Y., Tumminello, M., Madi, A., Gur-Gershgoren, G., Mantegna, R.N., Ben-Jacob, E.: Dominating clasp of the financial sector revealed by partial correlation analysis of the stock market. PLOS ONE **5**(12), 1–14 (2010). https://doi.org/10.1371/journal.pone.0015032
8. Ledoit, O., Wolf, M.: A well-conditioned estimator for large-dimensional covariance matrices. J. Multivar. Anal. **88**(2), 365–411 (2004). https://doi.org/10.1016/S0047-259X(03)00096-4
9. Mantegna, R.N.: Hierarchical structure in financial markets. Eur Phys J B—Condensed Matter Compl Syst **11**(1), 193–197 (1999)
10. Wes McKinney: data Structures for Statistical Computing in Python. In: van der Walt, S., Millman, J. (eds.) Proceedings of the 9th Python in Science Conference, pp. 56–61 (2010). https://doi.org/10.25080/Majora-92bf1922-00a
11. Millington, T., Niranjan, M.: Partial correlation financial networks. Appl. Netw. Sci. **5** (2020). https://doi.org/10.1007/s41109-020-0251-z
12. Oliphant, T.: NumPy: A guide to NumPy. Trelgol Publishing, USA (2006). http://www.numpy.org/
13. Onnela, J.P., Chakraborti, A., Kaski, K., Kertész, J.: Dynamic asset trees and black monday. Phys. Stat. Mech. Appl. **324**(1), 247–252 (2003). https://doi.org/10.1016/S0378-4371(02)01882-4. Proceedings of the International Econophysics Conference
14. Plerou, V., Gopikrishnan, P., Rosenow, B., Amaral, L.A.N., Guhr, T., Stanley, H.E.: Random matrix approach to cross correlations in financial data. Phys. Rev. E **65**, 066126 (2002). https://doi.org/10.1103/PhysRevE.65.066126
15. Preis, T., Kenett, D.Y., Stanley, H.E., Helbing, D., Ben-Jacob, E.: Quantifying the behavior of stock correlations under market stress. Sci. Rep. **2**(1) (2012). https://doi.org/10.1038/srep00752
16. Rand, W.M.: Objective criteria for the evaluation of clustering methods. J. Am. Stat. Assoc. **66**(336), 846–850 (1971). https://doi.org/10.1080/01621459.1971.10482356
17. Wang, G.J., Xie, C., Stanley, H.E.: Correlation structure and evolution of world stock markets: evidence from pearson and partial correlation-based networks. Comput. Econ. **51**(3), 607–635 (2018). https://doi.org/10.1007/s10614-016-9627-7

Extracting Characteristic Areas Based on Topic Distribution over Proximity Tree

Takayasu Fushimi and Emi Matsuo

Abstract Many photographs with location information are posted on the LBSN, and these subjects well represent the characteristics of the shooting location, so they are widely used for hotspot extraction. However, only famous tourist spots with a large number of posts are mentioned, and there is a tendency that the potential spots are not be focused on. In this study, we propose a method to extract POIs with a common feature distribution in photographs as areas and to characterize the areas by topics that appear more often in the area than in the surrounding area. Specifically, the minimum spanning tree is constructed from the position information of the posted photos, and the target region is divided into sub-areas by cutting the tree according to the feature distribution of the posted photo calculated by VGG16. An evaluation experiment using photographs taken in Tokyo shows that it outperforms existing methods in terms of semantic cohesiveness with similar feature distribution and positional cohesiveness with close shooting positions. Furthermore, compared with the feature distribution of the entire target region, the evaluation is made from the viewpoint of whether each divided area has a characteristic topic, and the photographs peculiar to each area are confirmed.

1 Introduction

With the advent of SNSs including Location-Based Social Networks, LBSN, many people post and share photos taken on social media such as Twitter[1] and Flickr.[2] Many of the posted photographs have location information attached, which means the subject of the photograph can be taken at that location, so it can be said that

[1]https://twitter.com/.
[2]https://flickr.com/.

T. Fushimi (✉) · E. Matsuo
School of Computer Science, Tokyo University of Technology, Hachioji 192-0982, Japan
e-mail: fushimity@edu.teu.ac.jp

E. Matsuo
e-mail: c011833521@edu.teu.ac.jp

D. Pacheco et al. (eds.), *Complex Networks XIII*, Springer Proceedings in Complexity,
https://doi.org/10.1007/978-3-031-17658-6_9

the subject of the photograph represents the characteristics of the area. When many objects of similar concepts in a certain area are photographed, the object is the highlight of the area and can be said to be a tourism resource. Some of these tourism resources are generally known, while others are not widely known, so it can be said that photos showing the potential appeal of the region are also posted. Now that the Internet has become widespread, even if it is not well known, it is spread on SNS, and people may gather at stores and tourist spots, and it may become a new tourist spot. Extracting the potential attraction of such areas is considered important for the further development of the tourism industry and the analysis of people's interests. Many websites on tourism present popular tourism resources in each region such as administrative divisions, but natural tourism resources such as mountains and rivers often span multiple administrative divisions, and potential tourism resources are not higlighted. Therefore, it is important to clarify what kind of characteristics there are by dividing the area according to the characteristics of the area regardless of the administrative division and annotating the area with the characteristics including potential signature.

To this end, in this study, by using geotagged photographs posted on SNS, we propose a novel method to divide the region into areas with common characteristics in simultaneous consideration of both the positional cohesiveness that indicates the vicinity of the posted locations and the semantical cohesiveness that indicates the similarity of the photograph features. More specifically, a positional cohesive tree is constructed by connecting nearby shooting locations (POIs) based on location information, and by cutting the tree at edges where the topic distribution is significantly different, areas with similar topics are extracted as each divided subtree (set of POIs). For each divided area, we quantify the degree of uniqueness that topics are significantly more abundantly distributed in the divided areas compared to the entire target region. Then we annotate each area by posted photos that have unique characteristics. If an appropriate regional division can be output, features that are unevenly distributed in that region can be detected and can be applied to regional branding. In small areas, the number of feature quantities distributed tends to be small overall, so the characteristics may be buried due to the difference in the number of distributions in a large area.

2 Related Work

This section describes the relation between our approach and conventional methods on community detection and graph cut and region division.

2.1 Community Detection and Graph Cut

Our method extracts cutting-edges in a minimum spanning tree constructed from POIs so as to cluster the POIs with positional and semantical cohesiveness, and thus can be treated as a community detection or graph cut method. Research on community detection is one of major stream of complex network analysis, and in recent years, many methods for community detection have been developed [3, 4, 6, 9, 11, 13–19, 21, 22]. Among these, Normalized cuts [19], GN method [9] and deep community detection [4] have a similar flavor to our method in terms of edge cuttings. These community detection methods partition the graph into densely connected subgraphs, and are effective for graphs where the difference between dense and sparse parts is significant, or where the degree distribution follows scale-free property, such as social networks with both high and low degree nodes. On the other hand, in the case of our target graphs constructed by connecting neighboring POIs, it is difficult to extract meaningful communities because the degree distribution generally does not follow the power law and the difference between dense and sparse parts is small. Moreover, the subgraphs divided by these methods are not semantically similar node groups, although they are groups of nodes that are positionally close to each other. Therefore, existing community detection methods are limited in their ability to detect node groups that have both positional and semantic cohesion.

2.2 Region Division

Studies on dividing a given geographical region into some functional areas or uniform areas have been conducted in geography. They are similar in terms of extracting certain areas with common characteristics. To extract these areas, multivariate and network analysis methods were proposed [1, 2, 5, 7, 10, 23, 24]. As a network analysis based approach, Zhang et al. analyzed topological structure of road networks and distinguished these structures into some patterns [24]. Though the study was based on the existing TAZ (Traffic Analysis Zone) delineation, Zhang et al. mentioned that how to decide the analysis unit is an important task and it should be studied as a future work. Farmer and Fotheringham applied the community detection method, which is proposed by Newman [12], to networks of travel-to-work flows, and found internally well connected and relatively cohesive regions [7]. In order to delineate urban boundaries based on human movements, Yin et al. adopted the community detection method, Infomap [18], to a directed weighted network, where nodes and weighted links respectively represent underlying urban regions and Twitter users' displacements on them [23]. In addition, a method has also been proposed that treats the urban road structure as a network and extracts functionally similar areas such as mountainous areas, residential areas, and commercial districts based solely on the topological structure of the road network [8]. Thus, the study of dividing regions into areas with common features has long been an important research subject that has been conducted across fields, but there has been no research on efficiently dividing regions based on feature and location information of a large number of photos posted on SNS and annotating each divided area with photos that have specific features.

3 Proposed Method

The purpose of this study is to divide the target region into subareas with different characteristics from adjacent other areas in terms of the topic distribution of the posted photos. For this purpose, the target region is divided into areas with similar features by clustering photos (POIs) with location coordinates and topic distributions, simultaneously taking into account both semantic cohesiveness, which indicates that the feature distributions are similar, and positional cohesiveness, which indicates that the location coordinates are in the vicinity.

Specifically, given a set of posted images (POIs) with location information $\mathcal{V}$ as input, our method divides the target area (set of POIs) $\mathcal{V}$ into K areas according to the following procedure:

1. Calculate the topic distribution $\mathbf{Y} = [\mathbf{y}_v]_{v \in \mathcal{V}}$ for all photos by VGG16 algorithm;
2. Construct a minimum spanning tree $G = (\mathcal{V}, \mathcal{E})$ based on the location information $\mathbf{X} = [\mathbf{x}_v]_{v \in \mathcal{V}}$ for all photos;
3. Cut the edges $\mathcal{C} \subset \mathcal{E}$ of the minimum spanning tree and segment into semantic and positional cohesive areas $\{\mathcal{V}_1, \ldots, \mathcal{V}_K\}$;

The VGG16 algorithm is used as a method to compute the topic distribution of the subject in the photo [20]. VGG-16 is a 16-layer deep convolutional neural network that loads and uses a network pre-trained with over 1 million images from the ImageNet database.[3] This pre-trained network outputs probabilities for classification into 1000 categories for the input photos. In this study, the feature vector of $v \in \mathcal{V}$ is represented by $\mathbf{y}_v = [y_{v,1}, \ldots, y_{v,H}]^T \in \mathbb{R}^H$, $(\sum_{h=1}^{H} y_{v,h} = 1)$, which is a probability distribution of the topics of the subjects of the photos. Topics are then selected for each photo until the cumulative topic probability in descending order exceeds a threshold value of θ. That is, arranging topics in descending order of topic probability $y_{v,h}$ and denoting $h(t; v)$ as the topic of rank t, we define the topic set of photo v as follows:

$$\mathcal{H}(v) = \left\{ h; \sum_{t=1}^{H(v)} y_{v,h(t;v)} > \theta \right\}.$$

Here, $H(v) = |\mathcal{H}(v)|$ represents the number of topics whose cumulative probability exceeds θ. With the VGG16 algorithm, $H(v)$ is small when a single topic in photo v is estimated as a high probability, but when the estimated probabilities are all low, many topics are assigned and $H(v)$ becomes large. In this study, we set $\theta = 0.8$.

---

[3] http://www.image-net.org.

Based on the location information $\mathbf{X} = [\mathbf{x}_v]_{v \in \mathcal{V}}$ of all POIs, an Euclidean Minimum Spanning Tree $G = (\mathcal{V}, \mathcal{E})$ is constructed. A spanning tree is a graph without a cycle, that is, a tree structure, in which any two points in space are connected by a straight line (edge) so that all points can reach each other via the edge. In particular, a tree in which points are connected so that the total Euclidean distance between directly connected points is minimized is called a minimum spanning tree. Therefore, a spanning tree with high positional cohesiveness is constructed because the edges are added between the POIs that are as close as possible. In this study, the target is points on a two-dimensional Euclidean space consisting of the latitude and longitude of the POI where each photograph was taken, and the photographs taken very close to each other is connected by an edge.

In a tree structure, when the number of nodes is $N = |\mathcal{V}|$, then $|\mathcal{E}| = N - 1$, and cutting one of the $N - 1$ edges splits the tree into two subtrees. To split a tree into K subtrees, we need to cut $K - 1$ edges. In this subsection, we select $K - 1$ edges $\mathcal{C} \subset \mathcal{E}$ of the minimum spanning tree so as to divide it into K semantically cohesive areas $\{\mathcal{V}_1, \ldots, \mathcal{V}_K\}$. Define an objective function for selecting edges to cut. For a set $\mathcal{G}_K = \{G_1, \ldots, G_K\}$ of subtrees divided by a set $\mathcal{C} = \{e_1, \ldots, e_{K-1}\} \subset \mathcal{E}$ of K edges to be cut, let $f_{k,h} = \sum_{v \in \mathcal{V}_k} \delta(h \in \mathcal{H}(v))$ be the frequency of the hth feature in the kth subtree and $F_k = \sum_{h=1}^{H} f_{k,h}$ be the frequency of all features. Here, $\delta(cond)$ is a Boolean function that returns 1 if the condition $cond$ is true. Now, in the multinomial distribution model where the feature h appears in the subtree G_k with probability $f_{k,h}/F_k$, the objective function is defined by the log-likelihood when the feature h appears $f_{k,h}$ times:

$$\begin{aligned}\Phi(\mathcal{C}) &= \log \prod_{k=1}^{K} \prod_{h=1}^{H} \left(\frac{f_{k,h}}{F_k} \right)^{f_{k,h}} \\ &= \sum_{k=1}^{K} \sum_{h=1}^{H} f_{k,h} \log \frac{f_{k,h}}{F_k} \\ &= \sum_{k=1}^{K} \left(\sum_{h=1}^{H} f_{k,h} \log f_{k,h} - F_k \log F_k \right) \\ &= \sum_{k=1}^{K} \phi(G_k). \end{aligned} \tag{1}$$

Here, $\phi(G_k) = \sum_{h=1}^{H} f_{k,h} \log f_{k,h} - F_k \log F_k$. We search for $K - 1$ cut edges $\mathcal{C}$ to maximize the objective function (1) and divide into K subtrees (areas). In this study, based on a greedy search algorithm with local search, we find one cut edge at a time that maximizes the Marginal Gain (MG) derived below. In the greedy algorithm, when choosing the $1 \leq k \leq K - 1$th edge $\hat{e}_k$, a cut edge is searched from each of the already segmented subtrees $\mathcal{G}_k = \{G_1, \ldots, G_k\}$. That is,

$$MG(e) = \Phi(\mathcal{C} \cup \{e\}) - \Phi(\mathcal{C}) = \phi(g) + \phi(\bar{g}) - \phi(G_i)$$

is defined as the difference between the function value $b = \phi(G_i)$ for the $1 \leq i \leq k$th subtree and the function value $b_g + b_{\bar{g}} = \phi(g) + \phi(\bar{g})$ for the subtrees $g, \bar{g} \leftarrow \text{divide}(e, G_i)$ to be partitioned when the cut candidate edge $e \in \mathcal{E}_i \setminus \mathcal{C}$ is cut, and the edge e for which $MG(e)$ is maximum is successively found from $\mathcal{E} \setminus \mathcal{C}$.

4 Experiments

In this study, we use photos with location information posted on the photo sharing site Flickr[4] between 2005 and 2019. The data includes the user name, user ID, title, tag, shooting date and time, posting location (latitude, longitude), posting time, and posted photo. In our experiment, we used photographs taken in Tokyo, and the number of such photos is 591,255. Our programs implemented in C++ were executed on a computer system equipped with Xeon processor E5-2697 2.7GHz CPU and 256GB main memory.

In this study, mean-shift clustering for latitude and longitude to output clusters with positional cohesion and k-medoids clustering for feature vectors to output clusters with semantic cohesion are used as comparative methods.

4.1 Visualization

First, we depict the visualization results of divided areas for each target region in Fig. 1. In (a) and (c) of each figure, the colored polygons are the extracted areas, i.e., clustered POIs, by our method and the MSC method; In (b) of each figure, POIs with the same colors are clustered the same groups by the KMD method, which are generally disconnected, so cannot draw polygons; In (d) of each figure, the colored polygons are city divisions; The gray border is the city division.

From Fig. 1a compared to the other results, it can be seen that the sizes of the extracted areas are not uniform, e.g., there are a large green area on the left side and many small areas on the right side. The left region is a mountainous area, where many photographs such as hiking and mountain scenery are taken, and the density of POI is relatively low. Whereas the right region is a metropolitan area such as Shinjuku, Shibuya, Harajuku, and Ueno, where many foreign tourists visit, the POI density is high and photographs of various subjects are posted. Reflecting these facts, it is considered that our method divided the Tokyo prefecture into such areas where similar photographs were taken.

Looking at Fig. 1b, it can be seen that POIs with similar feature vectors are scattered in the target area, thus this result is obtained because the KMD method does not consider the positional similarity at all. In more detail, in the left compared to the right of the region, there tend to exist POIs colored magenta but do not tend

[4] https://www.flickr.com/.

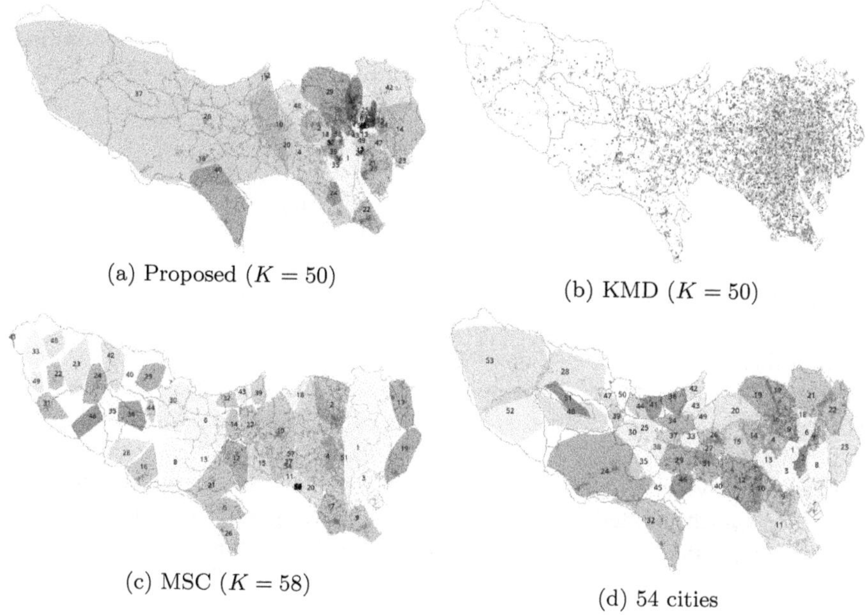

(a) Proposed ($K = 50$)

(b) KMD ($K = 50$)

(c) MSC ($K = 58$)

(d) 54 cities

Fig. 1 Visualization for whole region of Tokyo pref

to exist POIs colored blue and green. This tendency is consistent with the result of Fig. 1a where the left of the region is extracted as a large area.

The result of Fig. 1c is similar to the result of the city division shown in Fig. 1d, and it can be said that such a result is obtained because POIs located in the vicinity are extracted as the same area. The difference from the (d) city division is that areas with high POI density are extracted across administrative divisions such as cities, and this result is consistent with those of existing research.

4.2 Degree of Cohesiveness

This section evaluates our method in terms of the cohesiveness of extracted areas compared with existing methods. The positional cohesiveness of area $\mathcal{V}_k$ is defined by the average Euclidean distance between the coordinate vectors $[\mathbf{x}_v]_{v \in \mathcal{V}_k}$ and the coordinates of the gravity center $\mathbf{x}^{(k)} = \frac{1}{|\mathcal{V}_k|} \sum_{v \in \mathcal{V}_k} \mathbf{x}_v$:

$$\text{pos\_coh}(\mathcal{V}_k) = \frac{1}{|\mathcal{V}_k|} \sum_{v \in \mathcal{V}_k} \|\mathbf{x}_v - \mathbf{x}^{(k)}\|_{L2}.$$

We evaluate the positional cohesiveness by the average value over all divided areas $\frac{1}{K}\sum_{k=1}^{K}\text{pos\_coh}(\mathcal{V}_k)$. Similarly, the semantical cohesiveness of area $\mathcal{V}_k$ is defined by the average Kullback-Leibler divergence between the topic distributions $[\mathbf{y}_v]_{v\in\mathcal{V}_k}$ and $\mathbf{y}^{(k)} = \frac{1}{|\mathcal{V}_k|}\sum_{v\in\mathcal{V}_k}\mathbf{y}_v$:

$$\text{sem\_coh}(\mathcal{V}_k) = \frac{1}{|\mathcal{V}_k|}\sum_{v\in\mathcal{V}_k}\sum_{h=1}^{H} y_h^{(k)} \log \frac{y_h^{(k)}}{y_{v,h}}.$$

We evaluate the semantical cohesiveness by the average value over all divided areas $\frac{1}{K}\sum_{k=1}^{K}\text{sem\_coh}(\mathcal{V}_k)$. Note that, we define the cohesiveness by distance notion, so the lower these values are, the higher the cohesiveness in the divided area.

Figure 2 shows the degree of the positional and the semantical cohesiveness with respect to the number of divided areas ranging from 2 to 200, where red, green, and blue lines are the results of our method (PRP), the KMD method, and the MSC method, respectively. As for the MSC method, we cannot designate the number of divided areas, so the plotted value is limited. From these figures, for all the regions we used, we can see the following observations. As for the positional cohesiveness, the KMD method outputs a stably lower cohesiveness regardless of the number of areas, that is, the KMD method cannot divide the areas considering positional cohesiveness. This is because semantically similar POIs are dispersed within the target region and are not grouped together in a single area, as shown in the visualization results shown in Sect. 4.1. On the other hand, the MSC method and our method produce higher cohesiveness as the number of areas increases. It should be noted that the proposed method can divide the target region into areas with high positional cohesiveness as high as the MSC method. As for the semantical cohesiveness, the MSC method outputs a stably lower cohesiveness regardless of the number of areas, that is the MSC method cannot divide the areas considering semantical cohesiveness. On the other hand, the KMD method and our method produce higher cohesiveness as the number of areas increases. It should be noted that although the proposed method is not as good as the KMD method, it can divide the target region into areas with higher semantic cohesiveness than the MSC method.

From these results, it was confirmed that the proposed method can divide the region simultaneously considering both positional cohesiveness and semantic cohesiveness at the same time.

4.3 Degree of Uniqueness

This section evaluates our method in terms of the uniqueness of features distributed in each extracted area. Let $f_{k,h}$ be the appearance frequency of features h in the area $\mathcal{V}_k$, and let $F_k = \sum_{h=1}^{H} f_{k,h}$ be the appearance frequency of all features. The Z-score $z_{k,h}$

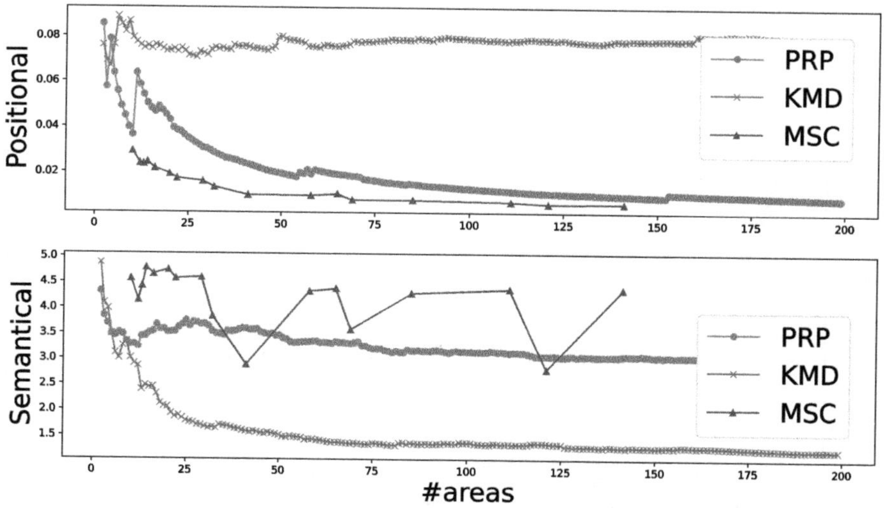

Fig. 2 Cohesiveness

is used to measure how much or less the actual appearance frequency $f_{k,h}$ is compared to the expected appearance based on null model $\hat{f}_{k,h} = F_k \cdot \frac{\sum_{k'=1}^{K} f_{k',h}}{\sum_{h'=1}^{H} \sum_{k'=1}^{K} f_{k',h'}}$:

$$z_{k,h} = \frac{f_{k,h} - \hat{f}_{k,h}}{s_{k,h}},$$

where $s_{k,h}$ is the standard deviation. The larger the value of the Z-score $z_{k,h}$ is, the more the feature h is unevenly distributed in the area $\mathcal{V}_k$, which means that the feature appears specifically in that area. The feature with the tth largest Z-score in area $\mathcal{V}_k$ is expressed as $h(t; k)$, and we evaluate the uniqueness of features by the average Z-score of the top T features over all divided areas $\frac{1}{KT} \sum_{k=1}^{K} \sum_{t=1}^{T} z_{k,h(t;k)}$. In our experiments, we set $T = 50$.

Figure 3 shows the degree of the uniqueness with respect to the number of divided areas ranging from 2 to 200, where red, green, and blue lines are the results of our method (PRP), the KMD method, and the MSC method, respectively. From these figures, for all the regions we used, we can see the following observations. The MSC method outputs a stably lower uniqueness regardless of the number of areas, that is, the MSC method does not divide the region so that a significant number of certain kinds of features appear. On the other hand, the KMD method and our method indicate higher uniqueness.

From these results, it can be concluded that the proposed method can divide the region so that each area has features that significantly frequently occur compared to other areas.

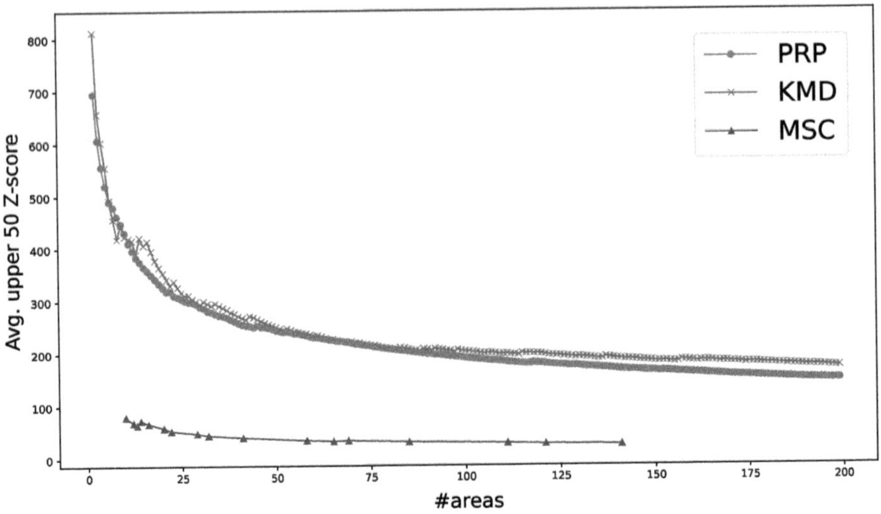

Fig. 3 Uniqueness

4.4 Representative Photographs

This section confirms the representative photographs in each divided areas. A representative photo is the one with the highest topic degree for the feature, which has a high Z-score value in each divided area.

Figure 4 exhibit the most representative photos in each of 50 areas extracted by our method, where the area numbers are consistent with those in Fig. 1a.[5] The following representative photos of Tokyo were selected: cherry blossoms, Tsukiji Market, baseball stadium, zoo, sunflower, Tokyo Metropolitan Government Office, Tokyo International Airport, GSDF station, pandas at the Ueno Zoo, Sanrio Puroland, and Sensoji Temple.

From these figures, it can be seen that areas with different characteristics can be extracted, and photographs that show the attractiveness of each area are selected. Some of these photos were taken at famous tourist spots, while others were taken by some core fans at potential spots. From these results, the proposed method permits the discovery of features unique to each area.

[5] Due to space limitations, representative photographs of all 50 areas could not be displayed, so 12 areas were selected at random.

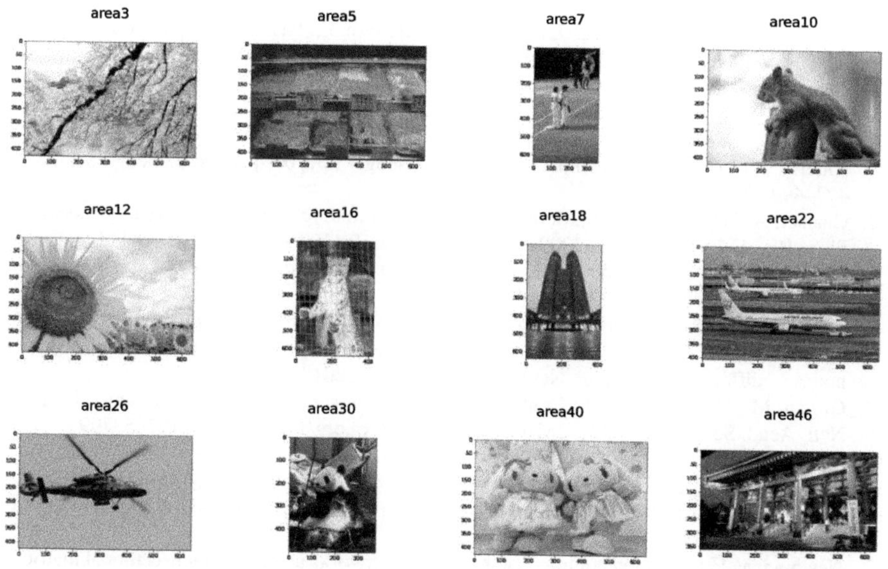

Fig. 4 Representative photos in divided areas

5 Conclusion

In this study, we tackled the problem of extracting characteristic areas with positional and semantical cohesiveness by proposing a method that connects POIs according to the taken locations and disconnects some of them according to the feature distribution of photographs. We conducted some experiments using photographs taken in Tokyo and showed that our method outperforms existing methods in terms of positional and semantical cohesiveness and uniqueness of features that appeared in each divided area.

In the future, we plan to extend our method to one that constructs other proximity graphs than the minimum spanning tree and divides them by general graph division algorithms.

Acknowledgements This material is based upon work supported by JSPS Grant-in-Aid for Scientific Research (C) (No.22K12279) and Early-Career Scientists (No.19K20417).

References

1. Berry, B.J.L.: Approaches to regional analysis: a synthesis. Ann. Assoc. Am. Geogr. **54**(1), 2–11 (1964)
2. Berry, B.J.L.: Interdependency of spatial structure and spatial behavior: a general field theory formulation. Pap. Reg.Nal Sci. Assoc. **21**, 205–227 (1968)

3. Blondel, V.D., Guillaume, J.L., Lambiotte, R., Lefebvre, E.: Fast unfolding of communities in large networks. J. Stat. Mech.: Theory Exp. **2008**(10), P10008 (2008)
4. Chen, P.Y., Hero, A.O.: Deep community detection. IEEE Trans. Signal Process **63**(21), 5706–5719 (2015)
5. Chen, W., Liu, W., Ke, W., Wang, N.: Understanding spatial structures and organizational patterns of city networks in china: a highway passenger flow perspective. J. Geogr. Sci. **28**(4), 477–494 (2018)
6. Clauset, A., Newman, M.E.J., Moore, C.: Finding community structure in very large networks. Phys. Rev. E **70**(6), 066111+ (2004). https://doi.org/10.1103/PhysRevE.70.066111
7. Farmer, C.J.Q., Fotheringham, A.S.: Network-based functional regions. J. Environ. Plan. Econ. Space **43**(11), 2723–2741 (2011)
8. Fushimi, T., Saito, K., Ikeda, T., Kazama, K.: Improving approximate extraction of functional similar regions from large-scale spatial networks based on greedy selection of representative nodes of different areas. Appl. Netw. Sci. **3**(18), 1–14 (2018)
9. Girvan, M., Newman, M.E.J.: Community structure in social and biological networks. Proc. Natl. Acad. Sci. **99**(12), 7821–7826 (2002). https://doi.org/10.1073/pnas.122653799
10. Grigg, D.B.: The logic of regional systems. Ann. Assoc. Am. Geogr. **55**, 465–491 (1965)
11. von Luxburg, U.: A tutorial on spectral clustering. Stat. Comput. **17**(4), 395–416 (2007)
12. Newman, M.E.J.: Detecting community structure in networks. Eur. Phys. J. B-Condens. Matter Complex Syst. **38**(2), 321–330 (2004)
13. Newman, M.E.J.: Finding community structure in networks using the eigenvectors of matrices. Phys. Rev. E **74**(3), 036104+ (2006)
14. Pons, P., Latapy, M.: Computing communities in large networks using random walks. In: Proceedings of the 20th International Conference on Computer and Information Sciences, pp. 284–293. ISCIS'05, Springer, Berlin (2005). https://doi.org/10.1007/11569596_31, https://doi.org/10.1007/11569596_31
15. Psorakis, I., Roberts, S., Ebden, M., Sheldon, B.: Overlapping community detection using bayesian non-negative matrix factorization. Phys. Rev. E **83**, 066114 (2011). https://doi.org/10.1103/PhysRevE.83.066114
16. Raghavan, U.N., Albert, R., Kumara, S.: Near linear time algorithm to detect community structures in large-scale networks. Phys. Rev. E **76**, 036106 (2007)
17. Reichardt, J., Bornholdt, S.: Statistical mechanics of community detection. Phys. Rev. E **74**, 016110 (2006)
18. Rosvall, M., Bergstrom, C.T.: Mapping change in large networks. PLoS ONE **5**(1), e8694 (2010)
19. Shi, J., Malik, J.: Normalized cuts and image segmentation. IEEE Trans. Pattern Anal. Mach. Intell. **22**(8), 888–905 (2000)
20. Simonyan, K., Zisserman, A.: Very deep convolutional networks for large-scale image recognition. In: Bengio, Y., LeCun, Y. (ed.) Proceedings of the 3rd International Conference on Learning Representations (ICLR2015) (2015). http://arxiv.org/abs/1409.1556
21. Traag, V.A., Waltman, L., v. E., N.J.: From Louvain to Leiden: guaranteeing well-connected communities. Sci. Rep. **9**(1), 5233 (2019). https://doi.org/10.1038/s41598-019-41695-z
22. Yang, J., Leskovec, J.: Overlapping community detection at scale: a nonnegative matrix factorization approach. In: Proceedings of the Sixth ACM International Conference on Web Search and Data Mining, pp. 587–596. WSDM '13, Association for Computing Machinery, New York, USA (2013). https://doi.org/10.1145/2433396.2433471, https://doi.org/10.1145/2433396.2433471
23. Yin, J., Soliman, A., Yin, D., Wang, S.: Depicting urban boundaries from a mobility network of spatial interactions: a case study of great britain with geo-located twitter data. Int. J. Geogr. Inf. Sci. **31** (2017)
24. Zhang, Y., Wang, X., Zeng, P., Chen, X.: Centrality characteristics of road network patterns of traffic analysis zones. Transp. Res. Rec.: J. Transp. Res. Board **2256** (2011)

Author Index

B
Balash, Vladimir, 97
Barnes, Matthew Russell, 15

C
Cardoso, Denis, 55
Cherifi, Chantal, 1
Cherifi, Hocine, 1
Clegg, Richard G., 15

D
da Mata, Angélica S., 55
Das, Bhaskarjyoti, 83
Diallo, Cherif, 1
Diop, Issa Moussa, 1

F
Faizliev, Alexey, 97
Farokhnejad, Sima, 55
Fushimi, Takayasu, 109

G
Gera, Ralucca, 69
Gholami, Saber, 29
Grigoriev, Alexey, 97

H
Harutyunyan, Hovhannes A., 29

K
Kapadia, Paritosh, 83
Kennedy, Sean, 69

M
Matsuo, Emi, 109
Melnichuk, Dmitriy, 97
Menezes, Ronaldo, 55
Molontay, Roland, 43

N
Nagy, Marcell, 43
Nicosia, Vincenzo, 15

P
Pechenizkiy, Mykola, 83
Pei, Yulong, 83

R
Rocha, Christiane, 55

S
Saxena, Akrati, 83
Sherrell, James, 69
Shields, William, 69
Sidorov, Sergei, 97
Smith, Philip, 69

W
Wish, Michael, 69

Z
Zakar-Polyák, Enikő, 43

D. Pacheco et al. (eds.), *Complex Networks XIII*, Springer Proceedings in Complexity,
https://doi.org/10.1007/978-3-031-17658-6

www.ingramcontent.com/pod-product-compliance
Ingram Content Group UK Ltd.
Pitfield, Milton Keynes, MK11 3LW, UK
UKHW020239061126
16351UKWH00016B/54
9783031176593